MAYER SMITH

The Secret Private Driver

Copyright © 2025 by Mayer Smith

All rights reserved. No part of this publication may be reproduced, stored or transmitted in any form or by any means, electronic, mechanical, photocopying, recording, scanning, or otherwise without written permission from the publisher. It is illegal to copy this book, post it to a website, or distribute it by any other means without permission.

This novel is entirely a work of fiction. The names, characters and incidents portrayed in it are the work of the author's imagination. Any resemblance to actual persons, living or dead, events or localities is entirely coincidental.

Mayer Smith asserts the moral right to be identified as the author of this work.

Mayer Smith has no responsibility for the persistence or accuracy of URLs for external or third-party Internet Websites referred to in this publication and does not guarantee that any content on such Websites is, or will remain, accurate or appropriate.

Designations used by companies to distinguish their products are often claimed as trademarks. All brand names and product names used in this book and on its cover are trade names, service marks, trademarks and registered trademarks of their respective owners. The publishers and the book are not associated with any product or vendor mentioned in this book. None of the companies referenced within the book have endorsed the book.

First edition

This book was professionally typeset on Reedsy. Find out more at reedsy.com

Contents

1. The Masked Chauffeur — 1
2. A Fiery First Impression — 8
3. Behind the Mask — 15
4. Rich Man's Dilemma — 24
5. Unexpected Rescue — 31
6. Journalist's Instinct — 40
7. Dinner Date Deception — 46
8. Sparks Behind the Scenes — 53
9. A Dangerous Secret — 58
10. Betrayal — 64
11. Confrontation — 70
12. Truth Hurts — 76
13. Love — 82
14. Fallout — 88
15. Redemption — 94
16. Apology — 99
17. Second Chances — 105
18. Grand Gesture — 112
19. Price of the Truth — 118
20. Shadows — 124

One

The Masked Chauffeur

The gleaming black Mercedes S-Class pulled into the circular driveway of the Carter & West Media office building, its tires rolling to a smooth halt against the pavement. Ethan Steele adjusted the cuff of his crisp white shirt beneath the sleeve of his newly acquired chauffeur's jacket, a stark contrast to the tailored suits he typically wore. His pulse remained steady, his breathing measured, but there was no denying the weight of the moment.

He was about to become someone else.

The irony wasn't lost on him—Ethan Steele, billionaire CEO of Steele Industries, a man who had been chauffeured around by professionals his entire life, was now posing as one. A driver. A silent presence in the background. It was a ludicrous idea, but one he had meticulously planned. He had watched from the shadows for too long as Sophie Carter, investigative journalist and media firebrand, painted him as the embodiment of corporate greed.

Sophie Carter—the woman who had spent the last three years tearing into the world of the ultra-rich, exposing corruption and exploitation with surgical precision. Her latest article, "The Billionaire Puppeteers: How Men Like Ethan Steele Control the World," had been a masterpiece of investigative journalism and a personal attack on him.

She didn't know him. But after today, he would know her.

Ethan flexed his fingers around the leather steering wheel. He had practiced for this—driving without arrogance, speaking only when necessary, keeping his true identity buried beneath the role of James Lawson, a private driver hired through an elite chauffeuring service. His assistant had arranged everything, ensuring Sophie's team would request a driver for the next month. She had no idea the man behind the wheel would be the very billionaire she loathed.

The glass doors of the media building swung open, and Sophie emerged.

Even through the windshield, Ethan could see that she carried herself with a sharpness that was almost militant. A navy-blue trench coat cinched at her waist, framing her lean figure. Her dark auburn hair was pulled back into a practical ponytail, but a few strands had broken free, framing her face. She was shorter than he had expected, but there was nothing small about the way she moved—deliberate, purposeful, like she had an invisible army at her back.

Her phone was pressed to her ear, her brows furrowed in irritation as she spoke rapidly into the device. She barely spared him a glance as she approached, reaching for the backseat door.

Ethan quickly exited the car, stepping around to open it for her.

Sophie halted mid-stride, her piercing green eyes flicking up to meet his. For a split second, there was a flicker of something—suspicion, curiosity, or maybe just mild surprise. He kept his expression impassive.

"You're new," she noted, lowering her phone slightly.

Ethan inclined his head slightly. "Yes, ma'am. James Lawson, at your service."

Her gaze lingered on him for a second too long, as if cataloging his features, weighing the authenticity of his presence.

"Where's Michael?" she asked.

"Your usual driver had an emergency. The company assigned me in his place," Ethan responded smoothly. His voice was lower than usual, his typically polished cadence replaced with the restrained tone of a man used to being in the background.

Sophie exhaled through her nose, clearly annoyed but too

The Secret Private Driver

pressed for time to argue. She slid into the backseat, and Ethan shut the door behind her.

As he returned to the driver's seat, he adjusted the mirror subtly, catching a glimpse of her as she resumed her call.

"Yes, Greg, I'm in the car now," she snapped. "We need to get the legal team to approve that exposé before we run it. I don't care if it ruffles feathers—when have we ever backed down from a story just because it makes powerful men uncomfortable?"

Ethan's jaw tightened.

The car eased onto the road, the purr of the engine the only sound accompanying Sophie's relentless dialogue. She spoke with authority, passion, and just the right amount of venom—like a woman on a mission to dismantle the empire he had spent years building.

"Look," she continued, "Steele Industries is practically drowning in offshore accounts and shell companies. And don't get me started on their real estate acquisitions—prime city blocks mysteriously getting rezoned after they buy in? That's corruption, Greg. The only reason no one's talking about it is because people like Ethan Steele own the conversation. But not this time. Not if I have anything to say about it."

Ethan clenched his grip on the steering wheel.

If she only knew the irony.

The Masked Chauffeur

The temptation to challenge her, to correct her, burned in his throat, but he swallowed it. This wasn't the time. He had come here to observe, to understand. To see the world through her eyes before he revealed himself.

A silence fell once she ended the call, and Ethan could feel her scrutiny in the mirror.

"You're awfully quiet, James," she remarked suddenly.

"Drivers should be," he replied.

She smirked. "Are you one of those 'seen but not heard' types?"

"It's usually preferable," he said, keeping his tone neutral.

She studied him for another long moment. "Where did you work before this?"

Ethan had anticipated this question. "Corporate driving. Some security transport work."

"Huh." She didn't seem convinced. "You look like you belong in a boardroom, not behind the wheel."

The irony was suffocating.

Ethan gave a small, polite smile. "Looks can be deceiving, ma'am."

Sophie tilted her head slightly, as if filing that response away for later analysis.

"Turn left here," she instructed, watching him closely. "Shortcut through the back roads."

"I have the GPS route," Ethan countered, though he obeyed.

"Yeah, well, sometimes technology doesn't account for traffic congestion," she murmured.

Ethan glanced at her in the mirror again. Sophie Carter was sharp, detail-oriented, and too observant for her own good.

The rest of the ride was tense but quiet, the only sound the steady hum of the engine. The moment they arrived at her next location—a downtown courthouse where she was covering a case involving corporate fraud—she wasted no time stepping out.

"Wait here," she instructed. "I won't be long."

Ethan nodded but didn't respond.

As she disappeared into the courthouse, he exhaled, gripping the wheel tightly.

He had spent years fending off journalists, crushing accusations, and handling media crises like a game of chess. But something about Sophie Carter was different. She wasn't just attacking the rich for the sake of a headline—she genuinely believed in her cause.

The Masked Chauffeur

And, to his own frustration, he was beginning to wonder if she had a point.

For the first time in his career, Ethan Steele wasn't sure if he was playing the game—or if he was about to lose it.

Two

A Fiery First Impression

Ethan sat in the sleek black Mercedes, his fingers drumming against the steering wheel as he watched the courthouse entrance. Sophie had been inside for over forty-five minutes, and he was starting to wonder if she had forgotten he was waiting.

His phone buzzed in his jacket pocket. A message from his assistant, Oliver.

OLIVER: How's the grand disguise holding up? Need me to send a real driver before she gets too nosy?

Ethan smirked but didn't respond. He had no intention of quitting his little experiment just yet.

A movement near the courthouse entrance caught his eye.

A Fiery First Impression

Sophie burst through the heavy double doors, her trench coat billowing behind her as she strode down the steps. Her jaw was tight, and her phone was clutched in her hand, fingers white from gripping it too hard.

Something had pissed her off.

Ethan barely had time to straighten in his seat before she yanked the door open and slid inside. The second she slammed it shut, she tossed her phone onto the seat beside her with a sharp exhale.

"Drive," she ordered.

Ethan arched a brow in the mirror. "Where to?"

"Just drive," she snapped. "I need to think."

He hesitated but shifted the car into gear, smoothly pulling away from the curb. The tension rolling off her was palpable, filling the car like an approaching storm.

Sophie pressed two fingers against her temple, eyes shut tightly as if willing away a headache.

Ethan wanted to ask what had happened inside the courthouse, but that wasn't his role. Stay silent. Stay in character.

But then she muttered under her breath, "Unbelievable. Absolutely un-fucking-believable."

The Secret Private Driver

That was enough to crack his resolve.

"Rough day?" he asked, his voice measured.

She snapped her eyes open, glaring at him through the mirror. "Do drivers usually make small talk?"

Ethan met her gaze briefly before turning back to the road. "Only when their passengers look like they're about to explode."

Sophie let out a dry, humorless laugh. "You have no idea."

"Try me."

She scoffed. "What, you're my therapist now?"

Ethan didn't answer. Instead, he let the silence stretch, waiting.

Sophie exhaled sharply and leaned back against the seat, staring out the window. Then, as if unable to hold it in, she spoke.

"I just watched a corrupt CEO—who we know was laundering millions—walk free because of some technicality in the case. A fucking loophole his high-priced lawyers exploited." She shook her head, her fingers clenching into fists. "People like him— they buy the system. They twist the rules. And no matter how much truth we dig up, no matter how much evidence we show, they always—always—find a way to escape consequences."

Ethan remained silent, his grip tightening on the wheel.

A Fiery First Impression

She had no idea she was practically describing him.

Sophie ran a hand over her face, her frustration pouring out in waves. "And the worst part? He had the audacity to smirk at me when he left the courtroom. Like he knew nothing would touch him."

Her green eyes burned with fury as she turned her gaze back to the road, her mind still lost in the injustice of it all.

Ethan knew the type of men she was talking about. He had shared boardrooms with them, shaken their hands at charity galas, watched them play the system like a rigged game. Hell, some of them had even done business with him.

The weight of realization settled in his chest.

Is that how she sees me too?

The thought unsettled him in a way he wasn't prepared for.

"Must be exhausting," he said finally.

Sophie glanced at him. "What?"

"Fighting against a system that doesn't want to change."

She studied him for a long moment. "Yeah. It is."

Ethan forced himself to focus on the road, but Sophie wasn't done.

"You wouldn't get it," she said, crossing her arms. "No offense, James, but guys like you? Chauffeurs? You work for the rich. You don't ask questions. You don't push back. You just... exist in their world."

He bristled at that but kept his face neutral. "And you think that means I don't see what goes on?"

She gave a humorless laugh. "I think you see exactly what goes on. You just know better than to care."

Ethan bit back a retort. He wasn't here to argue with her. He was here to understand her.

"Where to now?" he asked instead.

Sophie sighed, rubbing her temple again. "Take me home. I need to go through my notes."

Ethan nodded and smoothly changed lanes.

The rest of the drive was quiet, but the tension in the air remained thick. Sophie stared out the window, lost in her own world of thoughts and frustration.

Ethan watched her in the mirror, noting the fire in her expression, the way she clenched her jaw when she was deep in thought. She wasn't just passionate about her work—she lived it. Every injustice she uncovered burned through her like fuel, pushing her forward.

A Fiery First Impression

And for the first time, Ethan wondered if maybe… just maybe… she wasn't entirely wrong about the people at the top.

When they finally reached her apartment building, Ethan put the car in park and turned slightly in his seat.

"Do you need me to wait?"

Sophie shook her head. "No. I have everything I need."

She hesitated before grabbing her bag, as if considering something. Then, with a quick glance at him, she added, "You're different from my last driver."

Ethan raised a brow. "Oh?"

"He never talked. You do."

He shrugged. "Maybe I just like hearing people's stories."

Sophie studied him again, but this time, it wasn't just curiosity—it was suspicion.

"I'll see you tomorrow," she said finally, stepping out and shutting the door behind her.

Ethan watched her disappear into the building before exhaling a slow breath.

That was close.

She was sharp. Too sharp. And if he wasn't careful, she'd start asking the right questions.

But strangely enough, Ethan found himself looking forward to the next ride.

Because for the first time in years, someone was challenging the way he saw the world.

And he wasn't sure he hated it.

Three

Behind the Mask

The city pulsed with life as Ethan maneuvered the black Mercedes through the congested streets, the afternoon sun casting long shadows across the asphalt. His fingers curled around the steering wheel, his grip deceptively light despite the tension simmering beneath his composed exterior.

Sophie Carter sat in the back seat, her laptop open, fingers flying across the keyboard as she typed furiously. The soft click of her keystrokes was the only sound filling the cabin, apart from the rhythmic hum of the engine.

Ethan stole a glance at the rearview mirror.

She was in deep. Focused. Eyes narrowed, brows drawn in concentration. A lock of auburn hair had fallen from the loose ponytail she had thrown together, and she hadn't bothered to tuck it back.

He had to admit—there was something captivating about watching her work.

"James," Sophie said abruptly, not looking up.

Ethan snapped his attention back to the road. "Yes?"

"I need you to take a different route today."

He frowned slightly. "Your assistant already sent me the itinerary."

"Yeah, well, I changed my mind." She finally glanced up, her green eyes sharp. "I want to make a stop before the interview."

He hesitated. "Where to?"

"Jackson Heights. A warehouse on East 42nd."

That gave him pause. "That's not exactly the safest part of town."

Sophie smirked. "Did I ask for safety, or did I ask for a ride?"

Ethan exhaled through his nose, keeping his expression neutral. He didn't like this. He had read enough about Sophie's investigative work to know that she had a habit of walking into dangerous situations without a second thought.

But if he questioned her too much, she'd start getting suspicious.

"Understood," he said, turning onto a different avenue.

The silence stretched between them for a while before Sophie spoke again.

"You're not like the other drivers I've had," she said, closing her laptop and crossing one leg over the other.

Ethan kept his face unreadable. "No?"

She shook her head, studying him through the mirror. "Most of them don't ask questions. They just drive. You seem… aware."

"That's usually a good trait for a driver to have."

She tilted her head slightly. "Maybe. But it also makes me wonder."

He kept his breathing steady. "Wonder what?"

"If you're actually just a driver."

For a fraction of a second, Ethan's grip tightened on the wheel.

This woman was dangerous. Not in the physical sense—she wasn't a threat to him in any way—but in the way she noticed things. Saw through people.

The Secret Private Driver

He forced a small chuckle. "What else would I be?"

She watched him for a moment longer before shrugging. "I don't know yet. But I will."

That statement sent an unexpected thrill down his spine. He had spent years keeping people at arm's length, controlling narratives, ensuring that no one ever got close enough to see past the armor. And yet, here she was, poking at the edges of his disguise without even trying.

Ethan kept his expression carefully blank as they drove toward Jackson Heights.

By the time they reached the warehouse district, the skyline had shifted from glass towers to crumbling brick buildings, their facades scarred with graffiti. The air was thick with the scent of oil and asphalt, and the streets were lined with forgotten factories and empty loading docks.

Ethan pulled up outside an old warehouse, its rusted exterior giving away years of neglect. A group of men stood near the entrance, their postures relaxed but their eyes sharp.

Sophie grabbed her phone and tucked it into her coat pocket.

"I'll be twenty minutes," she said, opening the door.

Ethan didn't like this. At all.

"Sophie," he said, dropping the formalities for the first time.

Behind the Mask

She turned back, surprised by the way he said her name.

He hesitated. He couldn't tell her who he really was, couldn't explain why every instinct in his body was screaming at him to get her the hell out of here.

So he settled for the next best thing.

"Be careful."

Something flickered in her eyes—something that looked dangerously close to curiosity.

"I always am," she said, before disappearing inside.

Ethan clenched his jaw, watching as the men near the entrance exchanged looks before following her in.

Damn it.

He exhaled slowly, forcing himself to stay put. He wasn't supposed to intervene. He was just a driver.

But after ten minutes, his patience wore thin.

Something wasn't right.

Ethan killed the engine, stepping out of the car. He walked toward the warehouse, moving with an ease that betrayed years of training, years of knowing how to blend in.

The second he stepped inside, his instincts went on high alert.

Sophie stood in the middle of the room, arms crossed, facing off with a broad-shouldered man in a dark leather jacket. There were three others behind him, their expressions ranging from amused to unimpressed.

"Like I said," Sophie was saying, her voice cool and even, "I just need a statement. Then I'll leave."

The man in the leather jacket chuckled. "And like I said, sweetheart, we don't give statements to reporters."

Ethan's jaw tightened.

Sophie didn't back down. "So you'd rather I run the story without your side of things?"

One of the men took a step closer to her. "I think what he's saying is, you shouldn't be running any story."

Sophie's spine stiffened. "Is that a threat?"

The man smirked. "Depends. Are you smart enough to take the hint?"

Ethan's fingers curled into fists at his sides.

He knew Sophie was fearless. Knew she was the type to charge headfirst into a situation even when she had no backup.

But he was here now.

Ethan took a step forward, his voice calm but commanding. "Everything okay here?"

Sophie turned, her eyes widening slightly at the sight of him.

The men in the room tensed, assessing him.

Leather Jacket scowled. "Who the hell are you?"

Ethan tilted his head. "Just the driver."

The man let out a laugh. "The driver, huh?" He glanced at Sophie. "Didn't realize you needed a bodyguard now."

Sophie straightened. "I don't. He's leaving."

Ethan didn't move. His eyes flickered to her, and in that split second, an unspoken conversation passed between them.

You're in over your head.

I can handle it.

Maybe. But I'm not letting you do it alone.

Ethan turned back to the men, his stance deceptively casual. "If she's done here, we'll be going."

Leather Jacket's smile faded.

The Secret Private Driver

"You got a lot of nerve walking in here, driver," he said, his voice lowering. "You sure you know what you're doing?"

Ethan met his gaze evenly. "Yeah. I do."

Something in his tone made the man hesitate.

Sophie exhaled sharply. "This was a waste of time anyway," she muttered, brushing past the group.

Ethan followed, keeping his steps measured, controlled. He didn't turn his back on the men until they were both outside.

As soon as they reached the car, Sophie spun on him.

"What the hell was that?"

Ethan arched a brow. "Rescuing you?"

"I didn't need rescuing," she shot back.

He smirked. "You sure about that?"

Sophie scowled. "Unbelievable. You—"

She cut herself off, exhaling sharply before climbing into the car.

Ethan followed, sliding into the driver's seat and starting the engine.

As he pulled away from the warehouse, Sophie folded her arms, glaring out the window.

"You're a terrible chauffeur," she muttered.

Ethan's smirk deepened.

You have no idea.

Four

Rich Man's Dilemma

Ethan drove in silence, the city lights flashing past in a blur of neon and streetlamps. The tension inside the car was thick, almost suffocating, but he said nothing. He knew Sophie was fuming, her arms crossed over her chest, her foot tapping impatiently against the car mat.

The warehouse confrontation had rattled her—though she'd never admit it.

Ethan, on the other hand, was struggling with an entirely different problem.

She was reckless. Fearless to the point of stupidity. And yet, he couldn't shake the feeling that her rage was justified. She wasn't just stirring up trouble for the sake of a headline—she genuinely believed in what she was doing.

And the worst part?

She wasn't wrong.

He knew men like the ones inside that warehouse. Hell, he had done business with them before. Maybe not the exact men, but the type. Corrupt, ruthless, willing to do whatever it took to stay in power.

And Sophie Carter had made it her life's mission to take them down, one by one.

She suddenly let out a sharp breath, breaking the silence.

"I don't need a damn babysitter, James," she muttered.

Ethan's grip on the steering wheel tightened slightly, but his voice remained steady. "I never said you did."

She shot him a look through the mirror. "You didn't have to. You stormed in there like some white knight, thinking I was in danger."

"You were in danger," he countered, eyes still fixed on the road.

Sophie scoffed. "I can handle myself."

Ethan finally glanced at her. "Sure didn't look like it."

She turned sharply toward him, eyes flashing with irritation. "Excuse me?"

He sighed, already regretting his words. "I'm just saying, it doesn't hurt to have backup when you're walking into a situation where people clearly don't want you there."

She huffed. "I don't get the luxury of backup, James. That's not how this job works. I don't have a security team, or an army of lawyers, or some billionaire puppet master pulling strings to protect me."

Ethan's jaw clenched. Some billionaire puppet master.

If only she knew.

Sophie turned back toward the window. "I walk into places like that because no one else will. If I hesitate, if I show fear, they win."

Ethan understood that. More than she could ever know.

But what she didn't understand—what she refused to accept—was that these people played by a different set of rules.

The powerful didn't just win because they were rich. They won because they controlled the game.

And Ethan was one of them.

The irony of the situation was almost laughable.

A billionaire masquerading as a chauffeur, driving around the very woman who had made it her mission to bring people like him down.

He should have felt threatened. He should have been looking for a way to discredit her, to shut her down before she uncovered something that could be used against him.

But instead, all he felt was something he hadn't in a long time.

Curiosity.

Because Sophie Carter, for all her fire and fury, was not just a journalist.

She was a force of nature.

And for the first time in years, Ethan found himself wondering what it would be like to be on her side instead of the one being targeted.

The thought unsettled him.

He couldn't afford to think like that.

Not when everything he had built was on the line.

Sophie suddenly spoke again, her voice quieter this time. "You don't get it, do you?"

Ethan frowned slightly. "What?"

She turned to face him fully, her green eyes searching his face.

"You don't get what it's like to fight for something bigger than yourself," she said, her voice tinged with frustration. "To wake up every day knowing you're going up against people who could destroy you with a single phone call."

Ethan met her gaze through the mirror.

And for the first time, he let a sliver of truth slip through.

"I know more about that than you think," he murmured.

Sophie narrowed her eyes slightly, studying him. "Yeah?"

Ethan forced himself to smirk, deflecting. "Yeah. Ever tried dealing with the kinds of clients I've had to drive around? Trust me, they don't always like to play fair."

Sophie snorted, clearly unimpressed. "Oh, please. You don't even talk to half the people you drive."

He shrugged. "You'd be surprised."

She rolled her eyes. "Well, I can promise you this—whatever you think you've seen, it's nothing compared to the kind of corruption I deal with."

Ethan didn't argue.

Because he knew she was right.

She had no idea that the very kind of corruption she fought

against was the same world he had built his empire in.

And the worst part?

He wasn't sure he regretted it.

Because being at the top had given him everything. Power. Control. Influence.

But then why—why did sitting in this car, listening to Sophie Carter talk about justice and truth, make him feel like he was on the wrong side of the fight?

Ethan pushed the thought aside as they approached Sophie's apartment building.

As he pulled up to the curb, she sighed and rubbed her temples.

"Look," she said, her voice softer now. "I appreciate the… whatever that was back there. But next time, don't do it. I don't need you to get involved."

Ethan met her gaze. "Noted."

She hesitated for a moment, then nodded before grabbing her bag.

As she stepped out, she paused, looking back at him.

"You're a weird driver, James."

He smirked. "I'll take that as a compliment."

Sophie shook her head but smiled faintly before shutting the door.

Ethan watched her disappear into the building, then exhaled slowly.

He should have been relieved that the conversation was over.

Instead, he found himself gripping the steering wheel a little too tightly.

Because for the first time in his life, Ethan Steele was starting to wonder what it would be like to be one of the good guys.

And he wasn't sure if he liked where that thought was leading him.

Five

Unexpected Rescue

The city streets were alive with the hum of late-night traffic, headlights flashing like fireflies against the asphalt. Ethan kept a steady hand on the wheel, his jaw set as he maneuvered the sleek black Mercedes through the maze of downtown.

Sophie Carter was in the back seat, once again glued to her phone, scrolling through notes for her next article. The soft glow from the screen illuminated her sharp features, her eyes flicking across the text with fierce concentration.

He had been driving her for almost two weeks now. Two weeks of biting conversations, heated debates, and silent observations.

And in that time, something had shifted.

The Secret Private Driver

She still didn't trust him, but she was getting used to him.

That, in itself, was dangerous.

Ethan exhaled slowly, pushing aside the thought. He had a role to play.

He was just her driver. Nothing more.

Then, Sophie cursed under her breath.

Ethan flicked his gaze toward the mirror. "Problem?"

She huffed, shoving her phone into her bag. "I need to make a stop before going home."

He arched a brow. "At this hour?"

"Yes." She leaned forward slightly. "There's a source I need to meet. He's skittish, doesn't do daytime interviews."

Ethan's grip on the wheel tightened. "Where?"

"An alley off 12th Street."

Ethan almost laughed. "You're joking."

Sophie narrowed her eyes. "Do I look like I'm joking?"

He glanced at her through the mirror, noting the determined set of her jaw.

Unexpected Rescue

No, she wasn't joking.

And that was the problem.

"Sophie," he said carefully, "you do realize that meeting an unknown source, alone, in an alley, in the middle of the night, is the literal definition of a bad idea, right?"

She rolled her eyes. "You sound like my editor."

"Maybe your editor has a point."

She scoffed. "He's just covering his ass in case something happens to me."

Ethan exhaled sharply. "Maybe you should be covering yours."

Sophie didn't respond right away.

Then, with a sigh, she leaned back against the seat. "Look, I get it. It sounds bad. But I've done this before."

"Doesn't mean it's smart."

She smirked. "Are you worried about me, James?"

Ethan kept his expression blank. "I'm worried about having to explain to your editor why I let you walk into an alley and never come back."

Sophie shook her head. "You won't have to. It's a five-minute meeting. I get the information, and we go."

Ethan wasn't convinced.

But he also knew Sophie well enough by now to know that arguing with her would get him nowhere.

He sighed. "Fine."

Sophie grinned. "Knew you'd see reason."

Ethan wasn't so sure about that.

—

Fifteen minutes later, Ethan pulled the car to a stop at the edge of a dimly lit alleyway.

The neon sign of a nearby bar flickered overhead, casting eerie shadows along the brick walls. A lone streetlight buzzed above them, its glow barely penetrating the darkness.

Every instinct in Ethan's body screamed that this was a bad idea.

Sophie unbuckled her seatbelt.

"I'll be back in five," she said, reaching for the door handle.

Ethan's hand shot out, gripping her wrist before she could leave.

Unexpected Rescue

Sophie froze, startled by the sudden contact.

Ethan's voice was quiet but firm. "If you're not out in five, I'm coming in after you."

For a moment, she just stared at him, her green eyes wide with something unreadable.

Then, she smirked. "Didn't peg you for the overprotective type, James."

Ethan let go, leaning back. "I'm not. I just don't like loose ends."

She gave him a mock salute before slipping out of the car.

Ethan watched as she disappeared into the shadows.

Then, he cursed under his breath.

This was a mistake.

—

Five minutes passed.

Then six.

Then seven.

Ethan's patience snapped.

He threw the car into park and stepped out, his eyes scanning the alley.

Silence.

His gut twisted.

Ethan moved forward, his steps careful but quick, his ears tuned for any sound.

Then he heard it.

A muffled thud.

A grunt.

A curse.

His pulse spiked.

He turned the corner just in time to see Sophie struggling against a man twice her size.

Her back was pinned against the brick wall, her hands shoving at his chest as he leaned in, his voice a low growl.

"I don't like reporters sticking their noses where they don't belong."

Ethan didn't think.

Unexpected Rescue

He moved.

One second, he was a bystander. The next, he was slamming into the man with enough force to send him staggering backward.

The guy barely had time to register what had happened before Ethan's fist connected with his jaw.

The crunch of impact echoed through the alley.

The man crumpled to the ground, groaning.

Ethan didn't give him time to recover. He grabbed Sophie's wrist.

"We're leaving," he said sharply.

Sophie, still wide-eyed, nodded.

Ethan pulled her toward the car, his entire body coiled with adrenaline.

As soon as they were inside, he locked the doors and sped off, his jaw clenched.

Silence stretched between them, thick and charged.

Then Sophie exhaled shakily. "Well. That was exciting."

Ethan shot her a glare. "Are you insane?"

The Secret Private Driver

Sophie blinked. "Excuse me?"

Ethan's hands tightened around the wheel. "That guy could have killed you."

She scoffed. "He was trying to scare me."

Ethan turned sharply to her. "And it almost worked."

Sophie frowned, shifting uncomfortably. "I had it under control."

Ethan let out a harsh laugh. "Oh, yeah? Sure looked like it."

She crossed her arms. "I didn't ask you to save me."

Ethan slammed on the brakes.

Sophie gasped as the car jerked to a stop.

She turned to him, furious. "What the hell—"

Ethan twisted in his seat, his blue eyes blazing. "You shouldn't have needed saving, Sophie."

She opened her mouth to argue but hesitated.

Ethan exhaled, running a hand through his hair. "You think you're invincible. But you're not. And one day, your luck is going to run out."

Unexpected Rescue

Sophie swallowed hard.

For the first time, she looked… uncertain.

Ethan's voice softened. "Don't let it be today."

She looked away, biting her lip.

A heavy silence followed.

Then, softly, she murmured, "Thanks."

Ethan nodded, shifting the car back into drive.

Neither of them spoke for the rest of the ride.

But something had changed.

And Ethan wasn't sure if that was a good thing.

Six

Journalist's Instinct

Sophie sat cross-legged on her couch, laptop perched precariously on her knees. The faint hum of the air conditioner was the only sound in the room as she stared at the blinking cursor on her screen. Notes, transcripts, and photos littered the coffee table, each one a thread in the tangled web she was trying to unravel.

The adrenaline from the alley encounter had long worn off, replaced by a lingering unease that she couldn't shake. She'd told herself a hundred times that she could handle it—that she'd handled worse. But every now and then, she caught herself glancing toward the door, her senses tuned to every creak and shadow.

Her phone buzzed beside her, shattering the fragile quiet. She grabbed it, hoping it was the source she'd failed to meet. Instead, the screen displayed an unfamiliar number.

Sophie hesitated.

Every instinct screamed at her not to answer, but curiosity won out.

"Hello?" she said cautiously.

There was a pause, then a low voice spoke. "You're digging too deep, Ms. Carter."

Sophie's pulse quickened. "Who is this?"

"Someone who's been watching. You need to stop looking into Steele Industries."

Her grip tightened on the phone. "What are you talking about?"

"You know exactly what I mean. Back off, or there will be consequences."

The line went dead.

Sophie lowered the phone slowly, her mind racing.

She stared at the screen, her reflection distorted by the faint glow. She'd received threats before—plenty of them. Angry emails, letters, the occasional irate phone call. But this... this was different.

The Secret Private Driver

The voice was calm, deliberate, and disturbingly confident.

She dropped the phone onto the couch and ran a hand through her hair, frustration bubbling to the surface. She was on to something. She could feel it. And if someone was this desperate to shut her down, that meant she was getting close to the truth.

Sophie closed the laptop and stood, pacing the small living room. She needed more information, more connections, more evidence. If someone wanted her to back off, they'd have to do a hell of a lot more than make vague threats.

Her thoughts turned to James.

He'd been acting... strange.

No, not strange—just different.

Something about him didn't add up. The way he'd handled himself in that alley, the way he'd stepped in without hesitation and dispatched that thug like he'd done it a hundred times before. That wasn't the reaction of an average chauffeur.

And then there were the little things.

The way he spoke—polished, precise, as if he'd been trained to command a room. The way he carried himself—not like a man who spent his days waiting by a car, but like someone used to making decisions, to being in control.

Sophie stopped pacing, her arms crossed tightly over her chest.

Journalist's Instinct

She'd done some cursory research on him after that first day. The company that sent him seemed legitimate, and his name—James Lawson—pulled up a perfectly unremarkable background.

But now, she wasn't so sure.

Who the hell was he, really?

Sophie grabbed her laptop and opened it again, typing furiously. She sifted through public records, news archives, social media profiles—anything she could find that might hint at who James Lawson really was.

The hours ticked by, the dim light of her desk lamp casting shadows on the walls. Every lead came up empty, every search looped back to the same sanitized profile.

It was almost as if someone had gone out of their way to make him disappear.

Sophie leaned back in her chair, tapping her pen against the table.

There was something about James that didn't feel real. Something about him that felt... constructed.

Her phone buzzed again, this time with a text.

James: Picking you up at 8. Do you need me earlier?

The Secret Private Driver

Sophie stared at the message.

Her instincts flared again. This wasn't a driver checking in with his passenger. This was someone keeping tabs.

She typed out a quick response: 8 is fine.

Then she set the phone down and sighed.

If James wasn't who he claimed to be, then what was he after?

Her thoughts shifted back to the voice on the phone. The threat. The warning.

Maybe it was connected. Maybe James was more than just her driver. Maybe he was sent to keep an eye on her, to steer her away from Steele Industries and the truth she was chasing.

Sophie's jaw tightened.

If he thought he could scare her off, he had another thing coming.

She had a source to meet in the morning, someone who claimed to have dirt on one of Steele's top executives. If James was watching her, then he'd see her go through with it. He'd see that she wasn't backing down.

And if he tried to stop her?

Well, then she'd have her answer.

Journalist's Instinct

Sophie closed her laptop, her heart pounding with a mix of fear and determination.

Someone was playing games.

And she was about to find out who.

Seven

Dinner Date Deception

Ethan Steele tugged at his cufflinks, his polished reflection staring back at him from the mirror in his penthouse bathroom. The crisp tuxedo fit perfectly, tailored to his frame in a way that spoke of both wealth and power. He adjusted his bowtie and allowed himself a brief moment to consider what tonight might bring.

The gala at the Van Buren Hotel wasn't just another high-profile event. It was a strategic battlefield, a gathering of some of the city's most influential figures: CEOs, politicians, philanthropists, and media moguls. Normally, Ethan would stride into the ballroom as the commanding presence everyone expected him to be. But this time, things were different. This time, he had to be invisible.

Downstairs, parked outside his building, the black Mercedes

waited. It was a sight he'd grown used to over the past two weeks—though now it held an unexpected tension. Sophie Carter had called in a favor to cover the gala last minute, one she hoped would give her direct access to some of Steele Industries' allies. Ethan's allies. She had no idea that her chauffeur would also be attending, not as her driver, but as a guest who would navigate the event's social labyrinth under his true identity.

As Ethan descended the elevator, he couldn't help but recall her voice, sharp and questioning. He pictured her in the backseat, poring over documents, interrogating sources over the phone, and all the while, oblivious to the fact that the man driving her was one of the people she sought to expose. That had been the plan, after all: stay in the shadows, observe her, understand her.

But every time he was near her, the boundaries blurred. She wasn't just a fiery journalist with an axe to grind. She was brilliant, relentless, and in ways he couldn't quite admit yet—entirely captivating.

When the elevator doors opened, his polished façade was firmly in place. He stepped out into the lobby, his assistant, Oliver, waiting by the door with the night's itinerary.

"Everything's set?" Ethan asked, keeping his voice low.

Oliver nodded, handing him a slim tablet with a breakdown of the evening's guest list. "You'll be seated at Table Six with the city council representative and a few potential investors. Ms. Carter is assigned to the press pool, but she's been known to wander."

The Secret Private Driver

Ethan smirked. That was an understatement. Sophie didn't just wander—she infiltrated, observed, and dismantled. It was why she was so dangerous, and why he couldn't seem to stop himself from wanting to know more.

As he climbed into a different town car—one his own people had arranged—Ethan reviewed the names on the guest list. Each one was a player in the complex network of influence and money that Sophie had made a career of unraveling. Tonight, though, his challenge wasn't just about mingling and making deals. It was about staying one step ahead of the woman who would no doubt be scrutinizing everyone she encountered, looking for cracks, weaknesses, and secrets.

By the time he arrived at the Van Buren, the ballroom was already a dazzling display of luxury. Crystal chandeliers cast shimmering light across the marble floor. Women in elegant gowns floated through the space, their laughter mingling with the clinking of champagne glasses. Men in perfectly tailored suits formed tight clusters, their conversations laced with subtle power plays.

Ethan walked into the room with the ease of a man who belonged. Heads turned as he entered, some nodding in recognition, others quickly averting their eyes. He was used to it. His name carried weight, and his presence often shifted the dynamics of any room he entered.

But tonight, he wasn't looking for attention. Tonight, he was looking for her.

Dinner Date Deception

Sophie had already made her way into the gala, her credentials giving her access to most areas, though not the VIP lounges. He scanned the room, careful not to linger too long on any one face. Then he spotted her.

She stood near the edge of the room, a sleek black dress hugging her figure, her auburn hair swept into a low chignon. A press badge hung discreetly around her neck, and in her hand was a small notepad, the pen poised as if ready to capture the slightest slip of the tongue. Sophie wasn't mingling. She was hunting.

Ethan's pulse quickened, though he kept his expression neutral. He watched as she approached a group of executives near the bar, her posture confident, her smile polite but calculated. Within moments, she had slipped into their conversation, her questions light at first, but slowly growing more pointed. The men shifted uncomfortably, one of them glancing around as if hoping for a distraction.

Ethan couldn't help but admire her technique. She was relentless in the most subtle way—never too aggressive, never too obvious. Just persistent enough to make people nervous.

As much as he wanted to watch her work, he knew he had his own role to play. He moved toward his assigned table, exchanging greetings with a council representative and a tech mogul who had recently expanded into green energy. The conversations flowed naturally, the language of power and influence like a second tongue to him. But always, at the edge of his awareness, was Sophie.

The Secret Private Driver

She didn't notice him—not yet. To her, he was just James Lawson, her overly observant driver. She had no reason to look for Ethan Steele in the room, and he intended to keep it that way.

Yet, as the evening progressed, their paths inevitably drew closer. Sophie wandered from group to group, gathering tidbits, jotting notes, occasionally pulling out her phone to discreetly record a quote or two. Ethan kept his distance, careful to remain just outside her line of sight.

Then, during a brief lull in his conversation with the council rep, he saw her heading toward the VIP lounge. She wasn't supposed to have access. Her press badge didn't grant entry to that area. But Sophie had a way of finding cracks in the system. She moved with purpose, and the security guard barely gave her a second glance before she slipped through the door.

Ethan's chest tightened.

He needed to act.

Excusing himself from the table, he followed at a measured pace, keeping his steps light and his expression calm. As he entered the lounge, he quickly scanned the room. There she was, standing near a group of investment bankers who were deep in a low, intense discussion. Sophie stood on the edge, her notepad tucked into her clutch, her sharp gaze trained on them.

Ethan approached, careful not to draw attention. He leaned

casually against a nearby pillar, his eyes on the bankers but his mind on Sophie. She had no idea how dangerous this game could become. She thought she was just chasing a story, but if she pushed too hard, if she asked the wrong questions, she might find herself cornered.

A loud laugh erupted from the group of bankers, one of them turning slightly and catching sight of Sophie. The man's smile faded. He murmured something to the others, and all eyes shifted toward her. Sophie straightened, her expression composed but clearly aware that she had been noticed.

Ethan's muscles coiled. He watched as one of the men stepped closer to her, his tone low and threatening. She held her ground, replying with a calmness that only seemed to irritate him further.

This wasn't just a casual confrontation. These were men who didn't appreciate being watched, questioned, or recorded. And Sophie was standing in their territory, uninvited.

Ethan knew he couldn't stand by any longer. He moved toward her, his stride confident but unhurried, as if he belonged there as much as they did. When he reached Sophie's side, she turned to him in surprise.

"Ms. Carter," he said, his voice low and even. "I didn't expect to see you here."

Her eyes widened briefly, recognition flashing across her face, but she quickly masked it. "Mr. Steele. What a surprise."

The Secret Private Driver

The bankers exchanged wary glances, and the tension in the room shifted. Ethan's presence had changed the dynamic, and Sophie, ever the quick thinker, used it to her advantage.

"Well," she said smoothly, "I didn't mean to intrude. Thank you, gentlemen, for your time."

With that, she turned and walked away, and Ethan followed, the eyes of the room heavy on their backs. As they stepped back into the main ballroom, Sophie turned to him, her voice low and sharp.

"What the hell are you doing here?"

Ethan held her gaze, his face unreadable. "Keeping an eye on you."

She narrowed her eyes. "Why do I feel like that's not the whole story?"

Ethan smirked, though his voice carried a note of warning. "Because it isn't."

Sophie stared at him, searching for answers she wouldn't find. Then, without another word, she turned and disappeared into the crowd, leaving Ethan to wonder just how much longer he could keep his secrets from a woman who seemed determined to uncover them all.

Eight

Sparks Behind the Scenes

T he gala had all but concluded, and the ballroom had begun to empty, leaving behind the faint scent of champagne and expensive perfume. Sophie lingered near the bar, her notepad closed but still in hand, her eyes scanning the room like a hawk searching for one last piece of prey. Despite the initial confrontation with the bankers, she'd managed to glean a few critical leads—nothing earth-shattering yet, but enough to chase down.

Still, something gnawed at her.

Ethan Steele.

She'd known the man by reputation, of course—who hadn't? He was one of the most powerful and enigmatic figures in the city, a CEO whose fortune seemed to multiply with every passing quarter. She had built much of her career exposing people like him, peeling back the shiny veneer to reveal the corruption underneath. But meeting him in person? That had been unexpected. And unnerving.

He had stepped in just as things were about to turn ugly with the bankers. The timing had been too perfect, as if he'd been watching her. Protecting her.

Why?

Sophie turned the glass in her hand, watching the last remnants of her drink swirl around the edges. It didn't add up. She'd been working off the assumption that Steele and his ilk were her enemies—faceless titans of industry who would never lower themselves to notice someone like her. And yet, in the space of one evening, he'd not only noticed her but had gone out of his way to intervene.

Her gut told her it wasn't just coincidence.

It was a setup.

But who had set it up? And why?

She pressed her lips together, determined to find out.

As she set her empty glass down, a familiar figure appeared at her side. Ethan Steele, now without his bowtie, his shirt collar open just enough to suggest he was done with formalities, leaned casually against the bar. He looked at her, his piercing blue eyes studying her face with an intensity that made her want to step back—and lean in—all at once.

"Ms. Carter," he said smoothly. "Enjoying the evening?"

Sophie forced a polite smile. "It's been… enlightening."

He tilted his head slightly, a small, knowing smile playing on his lips. "You seemed to be making quite an impression earlier."

"Did I?" she asked, raising an eyebrow.

Ethan nodded, his gaze never wavering. "It's not every day someone gets the attention of men like that."

Her stomach twisted at the implication, but she kept her expression neutral. "I imagine they're not used to being asked real questions."

"Or being questioned at all," Ethan countered, his voice low.

Sophie turned to face him fully, her journalist's instincts kicking in. "Why do I feel like you're trying to tell me something?"

He smiled again, but it was different this time—almost amused. "Just an observation. People in my world… they don't take kindly to scrutiny. But you already knew that, didn't you?"

She narrowed her eyes slightly. "What exactly is your world, Mr. Steele?"

He didn't answer right away. Instead, he signaled the bartender and ordered a glass of whiskey. Once it was poured, he swirled the amber liquid thoughtfully before meeting her gaze again.

"My world is one of negotiations," he said finally. "Power, influence. Deals made in rooms much like this one, away from prying eyes." He took a sip of his drink, the motion deliberate. "And, on occasion, it's a world that overlaps with yours."

Sophie crossed her arms. "Meaning?"

"Meaning," Ethan said, leaning closer, "that you're poking around in places that tend to make people... uneasy."

"Uneasy," she repeated, her voice steady. "That's a polite way of putting it."

He smirked, setting the glass down. "Let's just say that unease often leads to... unintended consequences."

Her heart picked up speed, but she refused to let him see it. Instead, she tilted her head. "Is that your way of warning me off?"

Ethan's expression shifted, the smirk fading. "It's my way of reminding you that not everyone in this room plays by the same rules."

Sophie held his gaze. There was no overt threat in his tone, no raised voice or menacing look. But the implication hung heavy in the air. He wasn't trying to scare her, she realized. He was trying to protect her.

And that was the part she couldn't understand.

"Why do you care?" she asked bluntly. "What do you gain from warning me?"

Ethan's eyes flickered with something she couldn't quite name—something she wasn't sure she wanted to name. For a moment, it looked like he might tell her the truth. But then he stepped back, his polished mask slipping back into place.

"Consider it professional courtesy," he said smoothly. "After all, you and I have more in common than you think."

Before she could respond, Ethan turned and walked away, his broad shoulders cutting a path through the thinning crowd.

Sophie stood there, her arms still crossed, her thoughts spinning. He was hiding something—something big. And she wasn't going to stop until she found out what it was.

In the distance, Ethan disappeared through a side door, his confident stride never faltering. Sophie watched him go, her jaw set, her determination renewed. Whatever game he was playing, she intended to win.

Nine

A Dangerous Secret

The tension in Sophie's apartment was palpable as she sifted through the folders spread across her kitchen table. Each document was another piece of the puzzle, another lead pointing to what she suspected was a massive cover-up at Steele Industries. Her fingers moved quickly, flipping pages, circling names, making notes in the margins. Outside, the city buzzed faintly, a distant hum that reminded her she was far from alone in her search for the truth.

She was close. She could feel it. But the closer she got, the more the shadows seemed to close in.

Her phone buzzed on the table, making her jump. She snatched it up, her heart racing. A text from a number she didn't recognize appeared on the screen.

A Dangerous Secret

Unknown Number: You're digging too deep. Stop now, while you still can.

Sophie's blood turned cold. It wasn't the first time she'd been warned off a story, but something about this was different. This wasn't the vague, blustering threat of a PR team trying to cover their tracks. This felt personal.

Her hands trembled slightly as she set the phone down. She forced herself to take a breath, steady her nerves. Whoever it was, they wanted to scare her off. That meant they were afraid of what she might find. And that gave her an edge.

She leaned back in her chair, staring at the papers spread before her. One document in particular caught her eye: a series of transactions tied to an offshore account. The account was registered under a shell company that, on paper, had no connection to Steele Industries. But Sophie had traced the money trail back through several layers of intermediaries. The pattern was undeniable—millions of dollars funneling through the account at regular intervals, always linked to projects tied to Ethan Steele's empire.

She tapped her pen against the table, considering her next move. If she could prove the link, it would be a bombshell. Not just another exposé on corporate greed, but the kind of story that would shake the foundations of the company. It would put Steele and his associates under a spotlight they couldn't escape.

But it would also make her a target. More so than she already was.

The Secret Private Driver

Sophie closed her eyes briefly, exhaustion threatening to overwhelm her. She hadn't slept much in days, not since that run-in at the gala. Ethan's words had stayed with her, gnawing at the edges of her thoughts. He had been too smooth, too measured, as if he was playing a game she couldn't see. And yet, there had been something else in his eyes that night—something she couldn't quite define. A warning? A plea? She wasn't sure, but it had left her unsettled.

Her phone buzzed again. Another text.

Unknown Number: You don't know who you're dealing with. Walk away.

Sophie frowned, her resolve hardening. She typed out a reply before she could think better of it.

Sophie: I know exactly who I'm dealing with. And I'm not going anywhere.

She hit send and set the phone down. Let them know she wasn't afraid. Let them see that their threats wouldn't work.

But as she sat there in the dim light of her kitchen, surrounded by evidence that felt as dangerous as it was damning, she couldn't shake the feeling that she was being watched. The curtains were drawn, the doors locked, but the sensation lingered—a prickle at the back of her neck, a weight in the air.

Sophie pushed her chair back and stood, stretching her stiff muscles. She walked over to the window and peered through a narrow gap in the curtain. The street below was quiet, just a few cars parked along the curb and the faint glow of a streetlamp. Nothing out of the ordinary. She shook her head and let the curtain fall back into place.

Returning to the table, she grabbed her laptop and began to type. If someone was trying this hard to stop her, it only confirmed what she already knew: she was onto something big. And she wasn't going to stop until she uncovered the truth.

Her fingers flew across the keys as she compiled her notes, cross-referenced sources, and outlined the narrative. The evidence was there—it just needed to be pieced together in a way that no one could deny.

Hours passed. The city outside grew quieter, and the darkness deepened. Sophie barely noticed, lost in her work. She didn't hear the faint creak of a floorboard behind her or the subtle shift in the air. It wasn't until she felt the cold steel against her neck that she froze, her breath catching in her throat.

"Shut the laptop," a voice hissed in her ear.

Her heart hammered as she obeyed, her trembling hands slowly lowering the lid of her laptop. She tried to stay calm, to think clearly. This wasn't the first time she'd been threatened, but this was the first time someone had come this close. Whoever it was, they'd been watching her, waiting for the right moment.

"Who sent you?" she demanded, her voice steadier than she felt.

The voice behind her chuckled softly. "You ask too many questions, Ms. Carter. That's your problem."

She swallowed hard, forcing herself to stay composed. "If you hurt me, you won't stop the story. The files are already backed up. Someone else will publish them."

The pressure against her neck eased slightly, but the tension in the air didn't. "You think this is about a story?" the voice said, a hint of amusement in their tone. "This is about you not knowing when to quit."

Sophie clenched her jaw. "If you're going to kill me, just do it. But I won't stop. I can't."

There was a long pause, the silence stretching between them. Then the voice spoke again, quieter this time. "Maybe you're not as smart as I thought."

Before she could respond, there was a crash from the front of the apartment. The intruder jerked away from her, the cold steel gone from her neck. Sophie spun around just in time to see a dark figure fleeing out the back door, their footsteps fading into the night.

She stood there, trembling, her breath coming in short, ragged gasps. She didn't move, didn't dare chase after them. Instead, she grabbed her phone and dialed.

"James," she said, her voice shaking as soon as he answered. "Something's happened."

A Dangerous Secret

—-

What do you think? Any changes you'd like to make?

Ten

Betrayal

The sun was setting, casting a burnt orange glow across the city as Ethan pulled the black Mercedes into the underground parking garage of Sophie's building. He had come straight from a meeting with Steele Industries' legal team, where they'd been tightening the noose on several lucrative acquisitions. Yet, as the deal closed, his thoughts had been elsewhere. On her. On the woman who was, at that very moment, pacing nervously outside her apartment building, her phone pressed to her ear.

Ethan watched her through the windshield for a moment, studying the tension in her shoulders. She'd been jumpy for days, more guarded than usual. He wasn't sure if it was the threatening text she'd casually mentioned or the fact that her investigation was picking up dangerous momentum. Either way, Sophie wasn't the type to show vulnerability, which made

Betrayal

her current state even more unsettling.

When he stepped out of the car, she turned toward him, her expression a mix of relief and frustration. She ended her call and crossed her arms. "What took you so long?"

Ethan raised a brow, keeping his voice calm. "Traffic. What's going on?"

She glanced over her shoulder, then motioned for him to follow. "Not here. Inside."

Curious—and slightly concerned—Ethan followed her into the elevator. The silence was thick, but he knew better than to press her. Sophie only spoke when she was ready, and anything before that would just make her retreat further.

Once they were inside her apartment, Sophie bolted the door and turned to face him. "I need to know something, and I need you to be honest with me."

Ethan leaned casually against the counter, masking the unease her intensity stirred in him. "All right. Ask."

"Why do you always show up right when I need you?" she demanded, her voice low but sharp. "How did you know I was in trouble that night at the gala? Or when that guy tried to rough me up in the alley?"

Ethan tilted his head, meeting her gaze steadily. "Because it's my job to keep an eye on you."

Her eyes narrowed. "That's not the whole truth. I've been digging into you, James—if that's even your real name. There's nothing on you before you started working as a driver, nothing but a generic background that looks too clean to be real."

Ethan felt a flicker of admiration for her tenacity, even as his pulse quickened. "Maybe I'm just good at keeping my personal life private."

She took a step closer, her voice softening but gaining a sharper edge. "No. There's something you're not telling me. And I think it has to do with Steele Industries."

The words hung in the air, heavy with implication. Ethan's calm façade didn't falter, but inside, a storm brewed. He had known this moment would come sooner or later—Sophie wasn't the type to let unanswered questions linger. But hearing her say it out loud still hit harder than he expected.

"Why would you think that?" he asked, his tone carefully measured.

Sophie's lips pressed into a thin line. "Because the more I dig into Steele Industries, the more I realize that some of the documents I've found—some of the patterns—they don't just implicate the company. They implicate you."

She stepped even closer now, her green eyes searching his face for any sign of guilt. "So tell me, James. Who are you really?"

Ethan stayed still, his mind racing through possible responses.

Betrayal

He could deny everything, double down on the cover he'd so carefully maintained. Or he could admit the truth and risk losing any trust she might have in him.

"I'm exactly who I said I am," he replied evenly. "A driver who's seen too much and learned to stay quiet."

Sophie didn't look convinced. "You're lying."

Her words cut deeper than he expected. He'd been lying since the moment he took this job, yes, but there was something different about hearing her say it, about seeing the disappointment flash across her face. Ethan crossed his arms, his gaze steady.

"What do you want from me, Sophie?"

"I want the truth," she said firmly. "If you have nothing to do with Steele Industries, if you're not somehow connected to the corruption I've uncovered, then prove it. Give me something real, something that shows I can trust you."

Ethan hesitated. The irony of the situation wasn't lost on him. He was supposed to be the one watching her, understanding her motives, and here she was, demanding the same from him. But the stakes were too high. If she kept digging, she would eventually find something that would shatter her view of him entirely. And if she stopped digging… she might never know just how much danger she was putting herself in.

"I can't give you what you're asking," he said finally, his voice quieter. "Not because I'm hiding anything, but because I know you. Even if I handed you the truth on a silver platter, you'd tear it apart until it fit your narrative."

Sophie's jaw clenched. "That's not fair."

"Isn't it?" he countered, his voice rising slightly. "You see the world in black and white, Sophie. Rich people are villains, and everyone else is a victim. But what if it's not that simple? What if there's more to it than the headlines you write?"

She stared at him, stunned into silence. For a moment, the tension between them shifted, became something heavier, more personal.

"You think I'm being unreasonable," she said finally, her tone quieter but no less intense. "But you don't understand what it's like to fight this hard, to see how deep the corruption goes, and to know that most people would rather look the other way."

Her words struck a chord. He did understand, more than she could ever know. He'd been on the other side of that fight—building an empire that operated in those shadows, making decisions that blurred the line between right and wrong. And now, standing here in her apartment, facing her relentless pursuit of the truth, he realized just how much that world had cost him.

"I do understand," Ethan said, his voice soft but firm. "And that's why I'm telling you—be careful. The more you dig, the more you'll find yourself in over your head. And not everyone you

Betrayal

uncover will hesitate to shut you down."

Sophie's expression shifted, a flicker of uncertainty crossing her face. "Why do you care so much?"

The question hung in the air, and for the first time, Ethan didn't have an answer. He cared because she was relentless, because she was brave, because she made him see the world in a way he hadn't in years. He cared because somewhere along the way, she'd stopped being just another journalist and had become someone he didn't want to see hurt.

But he couldn't say any of that. Not yet. Not when his own secrets threatened to destroy what little trust there was between them.

Ethan straightened, pushing off the counter. "I'm your driver, Sophie. I care because it's my job."

Her shoulders sagged slightly, disappointment flashing in her eyes before she masked it. "Fine. Then drive me home."

He nodded and turned toward the door, his chest tight with everything he couldn't say. As they walked back to the car, he knew that tonight hadn't been a confrontation. It had been a warning shot. And whether Sophie took that warning seriously or not, the consequences were already in motion.

Eleven

Confrontation

The air was heavy with anticipation as Sophie stood at the edge of her balcony, the city sprawling below her. The faint hum of traffic, distant sirens, and the occasional burst of laughter from a bar echoed up from the streets. But all those sounds felt muted, drowned out by the storm raging in her mind. She clutched the small, leather-bound notebook in her hands—a notebook filled with everything she had discovered about Steele Industries, the shell companies, the offshore accounts, the whispered deals. The dots she had connected over the past few weeks were all there, each one leading back to the same name.

Ethan Steele.

And yet… it didn't make sense. None of it made sense.

Confrontation

She glanced at her phone, the screen lighting up with the time. 11:58 p.m. Two minutes until midnight. Two minutes until the man she once knew only as James Lawson—the man she had trusted, relied on, and even, in a way, started to depend on—would arrive to answer for his deception.

Her heart pounded against her ribs, her emotions swirling between anger and disbelief. She'd spent her entire career chasing the truth, exposing powerful figures who used their wealth and influence to exploit others. Ethan Steele was supposed to be just another one of them. But how could that man—the man who had shielded her from danger, who had given her subtle warnings, who had been by her side during some of her most vulnerable moments—also be the same man at the center of the corruption she had uncovered?

A knock at her apartment door broke through her thoughts. Her hand tightened around the notebook as she turned to face the sound, her pulse racing. She hesitated for a moment, every instinct telling her to stay back, to lock the door and keep him out. But she had to know. She had to hear it from him.

Taking a deep breath, she crossed the room and opened the door.

There he was. Ethan stood in the doorway, his tall, broad-shouldered figure silhouetted by the dim hallway light. He wore a dark suit, the tie loose around his neck, his usually calm, controlled expression marred by something that almost looked like regret.

The Secret Private Driver

"Sophie," he said, his voice low and steady, as though he knew exactly why she had called him here.

"Come in," she said, stepping aside.

He entered, his movements measured. Sophie closed the door and turned to face him, her arms crossed, the notebook tucked against her side.

"Why didn't you tell me?" she demanded, her voice trembling with a mix of anger and hurt. "Why did you pretend to be someone else?"

Ethan exhaled, his shoulders sinking slightly. "Because if I had told you who I really was, you never would've let me get close. You never would've trusted me."

"Trusted you?" She let out a sharp laugh, her eyes flashing with fury. "You lied to me! You've been lying this entire time, playing this… this role while I've been risking everything to uncover the truth!"

"Sophie, it wasn't that simple," he said, his voice still calm, but now tinged with something almost pleading. "I needed to understand what you were after, why you were so determined to come after me and people like me."

She shook her head, her jaw tightening. "So, what? You thought if you played chauffeur for a few weeks, you'd figure me out? That you'd convince me to stop digging?"

Confrontation

"No," he said firmly. "I never intended to stop you. I just... I wanted to see things from your perspective."

Her mouth opened in shock, but no words came out. She hadn't expected that response.

"I needed to understand why someone like you—someone intelligent, driven, and capable—would have such hatred for the people at the top," Ethan continued. "And the more time I spent with you, the more I realized that you weren't just doing this for a headline or a paycheck. You genuinely care about exposing injustice. About making a difference."

She blinked, caught off guard by the sincerity in his voice. For a moment, she faltered, the hard edge of her anger softening.

But then she tightened her grip on the notebook and stepped forward. "You're still part of that world, Ethan. No matter what you say, you're still the man behind Steele Industries. The man who profits off of the very corruption I'm trying to expose."

His jaw tightened, but he didn't look away. "I know. And I'm not going to deny that I've benefited from it. But it's not as black-and-white as you think."

"Then explain it to me," Sophie said, her voice rising. "Tell me why I should believe anything you say."

Ethan was silent for a moment, his expression unreadable. Then he reached into his jacket pocket and pulled out a flash drive, holding it out to her.

The Secret Private Driver

"What is that?" she asked, eyeing it warily.

"Proof," he said. "Of everything you've been looking for. The offshore accounts, the shell companies, the deals that never should have happened. It's all here."

She stared at the flash drive, her heart racing. "Why would you give this to me?"

"Because I'm not your enemy, Sophie," he said quietly. "And because you deserve to know the truth."

Her hand hovered over the drive, but she didn't take it. "What's the catch?"

"There's no catch," Ethan said, his voice steady. "I've seen what happens when people try to stop you. I know you won't back down. I know you'll get this story out, no matter what. So I'm giving you the evidence. Not to save myself, but because I believe in what you're doing."

Sophie's breath caught. For a moment, the room felt impossibly still, the weight of his words settling over her. She looked into his eyes, searching for any hint of deception, but all she saw was… honesty.

Slowly, hesitantly, she took the flash drive from his hand.

"Why now?" she asked, her voice barely above a whisper. "Why not just come clean from the start?"

Confrontation

"Because I was afraid," Ethan admitted, his gaze dropping briefly before meeting hers again. "Afraid of what you'd think of me. Afraid of what it would mean to let someone see the real me."

Sophie stared at him, her mind racing. She didn't know if she could fully trust him—not yet. But something in his voice, in the way he held himself, told her that he wasn't lying now. He was finally telling the truth.

She glanced down at the flash drive in her hand, the weight of it feeling heavier than it should. It was the key to everything she had been working toward, and it had come from the very man she had set out to expose.

When she looked back up, Ethan was watching her with an intensity that made her heart skip. She opened her mouth to speak, to say something—anything—but the words wouldn't come.

And for the first time since this investigation had started, Sophie didn't know what to do.

Twelve

Truth Hurts

The sound of Sophie's heels echoed sharply against the polished marble floor of Steele Tower's lobby. Late afternoon sunlight filtered through the massive glass windows, casting long shadows across the pristine space. She clutched her bag tightly, the flash drive buried in its side pocket. Every step toward the elevators felt heavier, each one pulling her closer to the confrontation she knew she couldn't avoid.

After last night's meeting with Ethan, she'd barely slept. She had spent hours poring over the contents of the drive he'd given her. The documents, emails, and transaction logs painted a damning picture of Steele Industries—confirming what she'd always suspected and, in some cases, far worse. But what shook her most wasn't the extent of the corruption. It was the context Ethan had provided. His explanation of the machine he'd inherited, the choices he'd made to stabilize it, the lives he claimed to have helped through deals that, on paper, looked like exploitation.

It was a nuanced, maddening puzzle. The pieces fit together, but the image they formed wasn't as clear-cut as she wanted it to be. Ethan had opened the door to the truth, but the truth wasn't simple. It never was.

When she reached the elevator, Sophie pressed the button with a trembling hand. The mirrored doors slid open, revealing the sleek, modern interior. She stepped inside, her reflection staring back at her—poised, professional, but undeniably anxious.

"Floor?" the attendant asked.

She hesitated, then squared her shoulders. "Top floor."

The attendant nodded and keyed in the code. As the elevator began its smooth ascent, Sophie gripped the rail for support. Her mind raced, replaying her conversations with Ethan. His calm, measured voice as he admitted to his role in the system. The raw honesty in his eyes as he handed her the evidence. She couldn't shake the feeling that he wanted her to expose Steele Industries—that he needed her to do it. But why? Was it guilt? A desire to reform? Or something else entirely?

When the elevator dinged softly and the doors slid open, she stepped out onto a floor that screamed opulence. Thick carpets, tastefully modern artwork, and a breathtaking view of the city greeted her. At the far end of the hall stood the double doors to Ethan's office. They were slightly ajar, and she could hear the low murmur of voices inside.

As she approached, her pulse quickened. She pushed the doors open and stepped inside, the plush carpet muffling her footsteps. Ethan stood by the floor-to-ceiling window, his hands in his pockets, gazing out at the skyline. He didn't turn around, but he spoke, his voice calm and steady.

"You found what you were looking for."

Sophie set her bag down on the glass coffee table, her hand brushing against the leather strap before letting it fall. "I found more than I expected," she said, her tone measured.

Ethan turned to face her, his blue eyes scanning her face. "And?"

"And now I have questions," she replied. "About you. About why you're doing this."

He moved to the sleek, dark wood desk and leaned against it. "Because it's the right thing to do."

"Since when do billionaires care about doing the right thing?" Sophie shot back, her words sharp. "You can't expect me to believe you're suddenly turning over a new leaf."

Ethan's jaw tightened. "You think this is easy for me? Handing you everything you need to dismantle my own company?"

"It's your company," she retorted. "If you wanted to change it,

Truth Hurts

you could've done it yourself. You could've fixed the corruption instead of hiding behind the scenes, letting it grow."

His eyes flashed, but he didn't raise his voice. "You think it's that simple? That I can just wave a wand and clean up decades of entrenched greed and backdoor deals? You have no idea what it's like—what's at stake. Thousands of jobs, entire communities dependent on this company. I've been trying to hold it together long enough to make changes without collapsing the whole damn system."

Sophie crossed her arms. "So you're saying you're the hero in all of this?"

"No," he said firmly. "I'm saying I'm trying. And you're the one who's going to make it happen."

She stared at him, her mind racing. The idea that Ethan wanted her to expose Steele Industries, to bring the corruption into the light, was both exhilarating and infuriating. He was using her. Guiding her. But to what end?

"You can't control how this ends," she said finally. "Once the story's out, it's out. You can't shape the fallout."

"I'm not trying to," Ethan said. "I just want the truth to come out. All of it."

Sophie took a step closer, her voice softening. "And what happens to you?"

He held her gaze, and for a moment, she thought she saw a flicker of vulnerability. "That's not your concern."

It was a simple statement, but it carried a weight that made her chest tighten. For all his power and wealth, Ethan Steele stood before her not as a billionaire or a CEO, but as a man who had made a choice to sacrifice his carefully curated empire. It didn't absolve him of his past actions, but it made her see him in a different light.

She glanced at the notebook on the table, then back at him. "You're risking everything."

"I already have," he said quietly.

Sophie turned toward the window, staring out at the city skyline. Her reflection ghosted back at her, alongside Ethan's. She felt the weight of the story she was about to publish, the lives it would impact, the chaos it would unleash. But for the first time, she wasn't sure if she was entirely in control of what came next.

"You know what this will do to your reputation, your legacy," she said.

"I know," he replied. "But legacies don't matter when they're built on lies."

His words hung in the air, and for a long moment, they stood in silence. Finally, Sophie turned to him, her expression unreadable.

Truth Hurts

"You might not come out of this clean," she said.

Ethan gave a faint, wry smile. "I don't expect to."

Sophie picked up her bag and slung it over her shoulder. "Then I guess we'll see what happens."

She started toward the door, her heels clicking softly against the carpet. Ethan's voice stopped her before she reached it.

"Sophie."

She turned, her heart skipping.

"Thank you."

For a moment, she thought about responding, about saying something that would lighten the tension between them. But she didn't. Instead, she nodded and left the office.

As the elevator descended, Sophie clutched her bag tightly. The flash drive inside felt heavier now, as if it carried not just the weight of her story, but the weight of Ethan Steele's strange, unexpected trust.

When the doors opened to the lobby, she stepped out, her mind already racing with how she would frame the narrative. This wasn't just another exposé. It was something far more complicated.

And it was up to her to tell it.

Thirteen

Love

Sophie stared at her laptop screen, the cursor blinking relentlessly at the top of the blank document. She'd already gone through two cups of coffee and countless drafts of an opening line, but nothing felt right. The room around her was dim, the soft yellow glow from her desk lamp barely cutting through the gathering gloom. Outside, the city was muffled by an approaching storm, clouds thick and dark, mirroring the storm inside her mind.

On the flash drive Ethan had given her was everything she needed. Every lead confirmed. Every loose end tied up. It was the kind of story that would cement her career, not just as a competent investigative journalist but as the one who took down one of the most powerful corporate empires in the world. Steele Industries wouldn't just be shaken—it would crumble. People would lose their jobs, board members would flee, politicians who'd been quietly supported by Steele's money would face intense scrutiny. The system would be exposed.

And Ethan Steele himself would be at the center of it all.

Sophie rubbed her temples, her mind racing. She'd spent the last three days reviewing the documents again and again. She knew them by heart now—every suspicious transaction, every carefully worded internal email that hinted at corruption, every offshore account designed to funnel money away from regulators' prying eyes. But every time she tried to start writing, something stopped her.

She closed her eyes and leaned back in her chair, hearing Ethan's voice in her head: Legacies don't matter when they're built on lies.

Why had he done it? Why had he handed her the keys to his own destruction? Was it guilt? A need to cleanse himself of the weight he'd been carrying for years? Or was it something more calculated—something she hadn't yet figured out?

The thought gnawed at her. Sophie prided herself on seeing through people's motives. She had made a career out of exposing the hidden truths behind carefully curated public images. But Ethan Steele had blindsided her. He had played the long game, hiding in plain sight, and when the moment came to reveal himself, he had given her exactly what she needed.

And yet... she couldn't shake the feeling that there was something more. A deeper truth just out of reach.

The storm outside finally broke, rain pounding against the window. Sophie pushed back from the desk and stood, crossing the room to stare out at the rain-streaked glass. The city lights blurred into a kaleidoscope of color, and somewhere in the distance, a siren wailed.

She thought about the people who would be affected by the story—people she'd never meet, whose lives would be upended. It wasn't just about taking down Ethan Steele. It was about everyone connected to his empire, everyone who had built their livelihood on what they believed was solid ground. When she pulled the rug out from under them, it wouldn't just be the guilty who fell. Collateral damage was unavoidable.

And then there was Ethan.

Sophie clenched her jaw, hating herself for hesitating. He was one of them. He had profited from the system, played by its rules, and thrived in its shadows. But she also remembered the look in his eyes when he handed her the flash drive. The raw honesty, the vulnerability he'd tried so hard to hide. He wasn't a hero, but he wasn't a villain either.

He was a man who had made mistakes—some monumental—and who was now trying, in his own way, to make things right.

Sophie shook her head, angry at herself. She couldn't afford to think like that. Ethan wasn't her friend. He wasn't someone she could trust. He had lied to her from the start, manipulated her. And even if he had handed her the truth in the end, that didn't absolve him of everything he'd done.

Love

But then why did she feel like she was about to betray him?

Her phone buzzed on the desk, breaking her train of thought. She turned and saw Ethan's name on the screen. Hesitating for only a moment, she picked it up and answered.

"Hello," she said, her voice careful, guarded.

"Sophie," Ethan said, his tone calm but with an edge of urgency. "Have you written it yet?"

She hesitated. "I'm working on it."

"I don't have much time," he said, his voice dropping slightly. "You need to publish it. Now."

"Why?" she asked, suspicion creeping into her voice. "What's changed?"

"Things are moving," Ethan replied. "Deals are being made behind the scenes. If you wait too long, they'll bury it all before it sees the light of day."

"And why should I trust you?" she snapped, her frustration bubbling over. "You've lied to me this entire time. What's stopping you from using me to take out your enemies while you walk away unscathed?"

There was a long pause. When Ethan finally spoke, his voice was quieter. "Because I want you to see the whole picture. The good and the bad. I need you to understand that even though

The Secret Private Driver

I've done things I'm not proud of, I believe in what you're doing. This story—it's bigger than me. It's bigger than Steele Industries. It's about a system that needs to change."

Sophie's throat tightened. "And what happens to you?"

"That's not important," he said, and she could almost hear the faint smile in his voice. "I made my choice the moment I gave you that drive."

She closed her eyes, trying to push away the lump forming in her chest. "You don't get to tell me what's important, Ethan. If I publish this, your career, your reputation—everything you've built—it's gone."

"I know," he said simply.

Sophie opened her eyes and stared at the storm outside, her reflection faint in the glass. She was a journalist. She had a duty to the truth, to the people who deserved to know what was happening behind closed doors. But for the first time in her career, she found herself hesitating. Not because she doubted the facts, but because she doubted her own motives.

Did she want to publish this story to expose the truth? Or was it to win, to prove that she could take down someone as untouchable as Ethan Steele? And if she did publish it, would it be justice—or revenge?

Her grip tightened on the phone. "You're asking me to destroy you."

Love

"No," Ethan replied. "I'm asking you to do what you've always done. Tell the truth. The rest is out of my hands."

The line went silent, leaving Sophie alone with the rain and her thoughts. For a moment, she stood there, the phone still pressed to her ear, as if waiting for something—some final piece of clarity that never came.

Slowly, she set the phone down and returned to her desk. The blank document was still open, the cursor blinking patiently, waiting for her to begin.

Sophie sat down, placed her hands on the keyboard, and started typing.

Fourteen

Fallout

The morning after Sophie's story went live, the world didn't just shift—it shattered. News outlets ran with it almost immediately, some citing her as their source, others scrambling to verify the mountain of evidence she had meticulously laid out. The headlines screamed of corruption, money laundering, and backroom deals that led straight to the doorstep of Steele Industries.

And, inevitably, to Ethan Steele.

Sophie watched it all unfold from her apartment, the television muted, her phone buzzing relentlessly with calls, emails, and messages from colleagues, rivals, and readers. She ignored most of them, focusing instead on the scrolling ticker at the bottom of the screen, which listed the names of board members stepping down, major contracts that had been frozen, and government agencies announcing investigations. She had known the impact would be significant, but this—this was a tidal wave.

And she was at the center of it.

Her own publication had run the piece as an exclusive, her editor calling her both a genius and a risk-taker. She should have felt triumphant, proud of what she'd accomplished. But as she sipped her coffee, staring at the screen, a hollow feeling sat in her chest. This was the truth she had fought for. The truth she had sacrificed sleep, safety, and, in some ways, her peace of mind to uncover.

So why did it feel so heavy?

Her phone buzzed again, this time with a name that made her breath catch. Ethan.

She hesitated, the weight of their last conversation still fresh in her mind. When she finally answered, her voice was carefully neutral.

"Hello?"

There was a pause on the other end before Ethan spoke. "I saw it."

Of course, he had. He was probably seeing it on every screen in every conference room, office, and public space he passed. His name wasn't just in the headlines—it was the headline. Sophie braced herself for anger, for accusations, but what came instead

The Secret Private Driver

was a calm she hadn't expected.

"You did exactly what you said you would," Ethan continued. "You told the truth."

Sophie set her coffee cup down, her grip tightening on the phone. "You don't sound surprised."

"I'm not," he said. "But that doesn't mean it doesn't hurt."

Something about the way he said it made her chest tighten. "You knew this would happen. You gave me everything."

"I did," he agreed, his voice quiet. "But knowing the fallout and living it are two different things."

Sophie closed her eyes briefly, her mind flashing to the image of Ethan as she last saw him—calm, measured, a man who seemed resigned to his own undoing. But she also remembered the man she'd known before that. The one who had stepped into danger to protect her, who had offered quiet words of caution when she needed them most. The two versions of Ethan seemed irreconcilable, yet here she was, talking to him, knowing she had played a part in dismantling everything he had built.

"I thought you'd be angry," she admitted.

"Why would I be?" he asked. "I handed you the evidence. I told you the truth. What you did after that was up to you."

She leaned back against the couch, staring at the muted TV

where talking heads were dissecting her article. "So, what happens now?"

"That depends," he said, his tone taking on a harder edge. "For me, it means my board is in chaos. My legal team is working overtime. Investors are panicking. For you…" He trailed off, as if considering his words carefully. "You'll be fine, Sophie. You'll probably win an award for this. Maybe a few."

She frowned, a pang of guilt twisting in her stomach. "This isn't about awards."

"I know," he said softly. "That's why I gave it to you. Because you care about more than the recognition."

Silence settled between them, heavy and charged. Sophie could hear the faint hum of traffic on his end, the world around him continuing even as his own crumbled. She thought about all the people who would lose their jobs, the ripple effects that would spread beyond Steele Industries' walls. And she thought about Ethan, sitting in his office—or wherever he was—watching his empire unravel because he had decided to hand her the rope to pull it apart.

"You had to know this would happen," she said finally. "All of it."

"I did," he admitted. "But knowing doesn't make it easier."

Sophie's chest tightened again. She hated that she felt for him, that she couldn't just see him as the villain she had always imagined. He was complicated, flawed, and—she could admit it now—human. That was the hardest part.

"What are you going to do?" she asked, her voice barely above a whisper.

"I'm going to face it," he said simply. "The consequences, the questions, the fallout. All of it."

She nodded, though he couldn't see it. "And you're not going to fight it?"

"I've done enough fighting," he said. "It's time for something different."

Sophie wasn't sure what to say. She had spent so long battling against powerful figures who never admitted fault, who always deflected, denied, and doubled down. Ethan wasn't doing any of that. He wasn't running, and he wasn't making excuses. It left her unmoored, unsure of how to feel.

When the call ended, Sophie sat staring at her phone, her thoughts spinning. She had published the truth, and now the truth was out there, unstoppable. But the aftermath wasn't as simple as she had expected. The fallout wasn't just about exposing corruption. It was about everything that came after—reputations destroyed, lives upended, a man she had come to know and respect being dragged through the mud.

The story had always been black and white in her mind: the powerful versus the powerless, the corrupt versus the honest.

Fallout

But now, in the aftermath, the lines felt blurred. Ethan wasn't the hero, but he wasn't the villain either. He was just a man who had made choices—some terrible, some redemptive—and who had handed her the truth, knowing full well what it would cost him.

Sophie glanced at the TV, where yet another panel of analysts was debating the implications of her story. Her name scrolled across the screen, praised by some, criticized by others. But all she could think about was Ethan's voice on the phone, calm and resigned, carrying the weight of a man who had accepted his fate.

And for the first time in her career, Sophie wondered if telling the truth was enough.

Fifteen

Redemption

Ethan Steele stood on the massive marble steps of his company's headquarters, flanked by a half-dozen stone-faced lawyers and a swarm of security personnel. Below him, a dense sea of reporters and photographers shouted questions, cameras flashing in a relentless barrage of light. The air buzzed with the tension of expectation, every person waiting for the man at the center of a corporate scandal to speak.

Ethan hadn't prepared a speech. He hadn't hired a PR consultant to craft the perfect apology or spin a narrative. He had simply decided that it was time to stop hiding. As he adjusted the microphone on the podium, the crowd noise began to die down, replaced by the eerie, almost unnatural silence of so many people holding their breath.

Redemption

"I know what you all want," Ethan began, his voice steady but heavy. "You want answers. You want an explanation. And you deserve one."

His eyes swept across the crowd, locking on a few familiar faces—seasoned journalists who'd been covering Steele Industries for years, others who had only joined the fray since Sophie Carter's exposé exploded across the media landscape. Somewhere in that crowd, Sophie was watching. He knew she wouldn't hide behind a screen when the truth she uncovered came out. No, she'd be here, ready to see how he would face the world she had turned against him.

Ethan gripped the edges of the podium, grounding himself. "The story you've all read—it's true. The documents you've seen, the accounts, the deals—they're all real. I won't stand here and deny what has already been exposed. I won't insult your intelligence by pretending otherwise."

A murmur rippled through the crowd. Ethan raised a hand to silence it. "But I do need to explain. Not to make excuses, but to give you the full picture. When I inherited Steele Industries, I inherited everything that came with it—the power, the wealth, and yes, the corruption. Decades of deals made before my time, partnerships formed in the shadows. I stepped into a system that was already broken."

Another wave of murmurs, but this time, they were quieter. Ethan pressed on. "When I realized how deep it went, I tried to pull back. I told myself I could fix it from the inside. That if I kept things running long enough, I could introduce reforms, make changes without collapsing the company, without putting tens of thousands of people out of work. But the truth is, I didn't act fast enough. I let the system continue, even as I made small steps toward change. I let the machine run because I was afraid of what would happen if I stopped it."

He glanced down for a moment, gathering his thoughts. "That was my failing. My fear, my hesitation—it allowed things to fester. And for that, I am deeply sorry."

The silence was heavy now, the crowd's initial hostility giving way to a tense, uncertain curiosity. Ethan let it linger before continuing.

"I've spent the last few weeks thinking about what redemption looks like," he said. "And I know that I can't simply stand here and tell you I've changed. Words mean nothing without action. That's why, as of today, I'm stepping down as CEO of Steele Industries."

The crowd erupted. Reporters shouted questions, microphones thrust toward him, camera shutters clicking furiously. Ethan held up both hands, motioning for calm.

"This isn't about saving my reputation," he said, his voice firm enough to cut through the noise. "It's about doing what's right. Steele Industries needs leadership that's not tethered to its past. It needs a new direction, and I'm not the person to guide it anymore. I'll be working closely with a transition team to ensure that the company moves forward transparently and ethically. And I'll cooperate fully with any and all investigations."

Another reporter yelled a question, but Ethan ignored it, focusing instead on the thought that had kept him awake for countless nights. "I'm also committing myself to addressing the damage caused. There are communities that have suffered because of decisions made by my company. There are lives that have been affected in ways that can't be undone. I can't change the past, but I can work toward making amends. I'll be funding initiatives aimed at rebuilding those communities and providing support for those who were wronged."

He paused, his eyes scanning the crowd again, looking for her. He didn't see Sophie, but he knew she was there, watching, listening. "And finally," he said, his voice softer now, "I want to thank the journalists who brought these issues to light. It's not easy to challenge those in power, to dig for the truth when every door is slammed in your face. But that's exactly what journalism is supposed to be. Holding power accountable. For that, I'm grateful. Even if it's cost me everything."

Ethan stepped back from the podium, ignoring the barrage of questions that followed. Security and his lawyers formed a protective bubble around him as he descended the steps, the camera flashes relentless. He felt the weight of their stares, their judgments. He didn't expect forgiveness or sympathy. He expected to face consequences.

As he reached the waiting car, Ethan stopped and looked back. The crowd continued to swell, the noise a chaotic swirl of voices and questions. He spotted a familiar silhouette at the edge of the throng, a figure standing apart from the rest. Sophie.

Their eyes met, just for a moment. In her gaze, he didn't see triumph or vindication. He saw something else—something quieter, more complex. Understanding, maybe. Or respect.

He nodded to her, a silent acknowledgment of everything that had passed between them. Then he turned, stepped into the car, and let the door close behind him.

The city moved on, but the fallout was far from over.

Sixteen

Apology

The crisp morning air clung to Ethan Steele as he stepped out of the town car, his polished shoes crunching against the gravel of the small community center's parking lot. For a moment, he paused, tugging his scarf tighter against the chill. The center wasn't much to look at—just a simple brick building with peeling paint around the windows and a faded sign hanging slightly askew above the entrance. But to Ethan, it loomed like a monument to everything he'd failed to see.

A handful of people were already gathered inside. He could see them through the wide, dirt-streaked windows—mothers cradling young children, older men slumped in worn chairs, faces weathered by time and disappointment. These were the workers who had been hit hardest by Steele Industries' quiet acquisition of their town's main factory. A factory that, under his watch, had been quietly shut down, its equipment shipped overseas, leaving hundreds jobless and a once-thriving community in ruins.

Ethan had read the reports, had seen the numbers on spreadsheets. But it wasn't until he stood here, on the ground where those cold decisions had unraveled lives, that the weight of his actions fully registered.

He drew in a slow breath and pushed open the doors.

The low murmur of voices inside stilled as soon as he entered. Heads turned. Conversations stopped. A woman holding a toddler on her hip looked at him with a mixture of surprise and suspicion. An older man with a cane stared openly, his lips pressing into a thin line.

Ethan stepped into the room, his gaze sweeping over the faces watching him. For a brief, uncharacteristic moment, his usual calm confidence faltered. These weren't the polished board members or sharp-tongued executives he was used to facing. These were real people.

One of them, a wiry man with gray at his temples and grease-stained hands, finally broke the silence. "You lost, Steele?"

The question wasn't said with malice, but it wasn't exactly welcoming either. The tension in the room was palpable, the unspoken resentment hanging heavy.

"No," Ethan said, his voice steady. He stepped further into the

Apology

room, unbuttoning his coat. "I'm exactly where I need to be."

The wiry man—he recognized him now as Roy Holloway, a former maintenance supervisor—crossed his arms. "Well, that's a first."

A few chuckles rippled through the crowd, but it was more bitter than humorous.

Ethan met Roy's gaze. "I'm here because I owe all of you an apology."

A low murmur spread, skeptical, almost disbelieving.

Roy raised an eyebrow. "Is that right?"

Ethan nodded. "I should have been here years ago. I should have been here before the factory closed, before the jobs disappeared, before families had to pack up and leave everything behind."

He turned slightly, addressing the entire room now. "When I took over Steele Industries, I thought I could fix things quietly. Make changes without anyone noticing, without disrupting the status quo. I told myself I was protecting the company, protecting livelihoods. But the truth is, I wasn't protecting anyone. I was keeping myself comfortable. I didn't want to make waves. I didn't want to take risks that could cost me everything. And because of that, I let the factory shut down without a fight. I let this community suffer."

Roy's jaw tightened, but he said nothing.

Ethan continued, his voice carrying more weight. "I can't undo what's been done. I can't bring back the factory or erase the years of struggle. But I can own up to my part in it. I can stand here and tell you that I was wrong. And I'm sorry."

Silence.

Then, a woman in the back—a young mother with dark circles under her eyes—spoke up. "Sorry doesn't pay the bills, Mr. Steele."

"I know," Ethan replied without hesitation. "And I'm not just here to say sorry. I'm here because I want to help rebuild. I want to invest in this community, to create new opportunities. It won't be easy, and it won't happen overnight. But I'm willing to listen. To work with you. To find solutions that actually help."

Roy's arms uncrossed, his expression shifting slightly. "And why should we believe you?"

Ethan looked him in the eye. "You shouldn't. Not yet. But give me a chance to prove it. Hold me accountable. Make me earn your trust."

The room was still for a long moment. Then Roy let out a short breath and stepped forward, his cane clicking against the floor. He stopped just a foot away from Ethan, looking him over like he was inspecting a machine part.

"You're serious about this?" Roy asked, his tone skeptical but

Apology

less harsh.

Ethan nodded. "I am."

Roy studied him a moment longer, then gave a small, almost reluctant nod. "We'll see."

It wasn't much, but it was a start.

As the tension in the room began to ease, conversations picked up again, quieter this time. A few people approached Ethan, cautiously asking questions, voicing concerns. He listened, nodding, taking mental notes. He didn't have all the answers yet, but he knew one thing: this was the beginning of a long road. One he had to walk if he was going to make amends.

When the crowd started thinning, Roy lingered near the door. As Ethan reached for his coat, the older man spoke up again.

"You could've stayed in your tower," Roy said. "Would've been easier."

Ethan paused, meeting his gaze. "It wouldn't have been right."

Roy grunted, a faint smile tugging at the corner of his mouth. "Well, you're here now. Let's see if you can back up your words."

"I plan to," Ethan said, his voice firm.

As he stepped outside, the cold air hit him again, but it didn't feel as sharp this time. He felt lighter, though he knew the hard work was only just beginning. He had taken the first step. The rest would be earned, day by day, through actions, not words.

He looked out at the small, quiet town stretching beyond the community center's parking lot. There were still so many broken pieces to pick up, so many people to help. But he would face it all head-on.

Because for the first time in years, Ethan Steele felt like he was doing something that truly mattered.

Seventeen

Second Chances

Ethan Steele arrived at the charity gala with none of his usual entourage. The driver he'd hired—someone nondescript, a far cry from the polished professionals who used to wait on his every whim—pulled the plain black sedan into the circular driveway, stopping just short of the red carpet. The valet opened his door, but Ethan hesitated before stepping out.

This wasn't his scene anymore. At one time, he'd have emerged with an easy smile and an air of practiced detachment, nodding at photographers, exchanging banter with the event's host, and gliding into the ballroom where the city's elite drank champagne and made deals over hors d'oeuvres. But tonight, he felt more like an intruder than a guest. He wasn't coming here to network, to make connections, or to close a deal. He was here for her.

The Secret Private Driver

Sophie Carter.

His breath fogged in the cold air as he finally stepped out of the car. The light drizzle did little to dampen the flash of cameras as they caught sight of him. The press had not forgotten his name, even if he'd done his best to step out of the spotlight over the last few months. Questions were shouted, but he ignored them, walking briskly toward the doors. His tuxedo, though still impeccably tailored, felt like a costume he no longer belonged in.

The moment he stepped into the ballroom, Ethan felt the weight of a hundred pairs of eyes on him. Some were curious, others openly hostile. The fallout from Sophie's exposé had been seismic, and though he had stepped down as CEO, the repercussions were still rippling through the industry. He'd been praised by some for cooperating with investigations, for acknowledging the company's wrongdoing. But others saw his actions as too little, too late. And here, in a room filled with people who had once been his peers, allies, and competitors, he could feel the unspoken questions hovering in the air: What is he doing here? What does he want?

Ethan moved through the crowd with purpose, scanning the room for Sophie. It didn't take long to find her.

She stood near the far wall, just outside the circle of luminaries who'd gathered to bask in their own influence. Her black gown was simple but elegant, a stark contrast to the shimmering, extravagant outfits that surrounded her. Her hair was swept back, exposing the sharp line of her jaw and the glint of her earrings. She looked poised, confident—yet detached. While everyone else seemed eager to be seen, Sophie remained at the edge, observing, taking in everything.

Ethan's pulse quickened as he started toward her. He hadn't seen her in person since the day he handed her the flash drive that had changed everything. Their brief conversations since had been over the phone or through intermediaries, always short, always professional. Now, standing in the same room again, he felt the weight of all that had passed between them.

"Sophie," he said softly as he reached her.

She turned, her green eyes widening slightly before narrowing with suspicion. "Ethan." Her voice was cool, measured. "What are you doing here?"

He gave a faint smile. "I was invited."

She raised an eyebrow. "Really?"

"Yes," he said, a hint of humor breaking through. "Believe it or not, not everyone has written me off."

Sophie crossed her arms, her gaze sharp. "And you came because…?"

"Because I wanted to see you," he admitted.

For a moment, Sophie said nothing. Her expression remained guarded, but there was a flicker of something—curiosity, maybe, or uncertainty. She tilted her head slightly. "You've seen me. Now what?"

Ethan hesitated. This was the moment he'd been turning over in his mind for weeks. He'd been rehearsing what to say, how to explain why he needed her to hear him out. But all those carefully planned words seemed to vanish as she stood before him, her presence challenging him in ways no one else ever had.

"I wanted to tell you that I understand why you did what you did," he said finally. "And I don't hold it against you."

Her jaw tightened, but she didn't look away. "You shouldn't. I did my job. That's it."

"You did more than that," he said. "You showed me something I hadn't been willing to see. You exposed what needed to be exposed."

"And it cost you," Sophie said, her tone flat. "You're not trying to make me feel bad about that, are you?"

"Not at all," Ethan said quickly. "I just... I want you to know that I respect you for it. For standing your ground. For not backing down. I've spent my life in a world where power silences truth, and you didn't let that happen. That matters to me."

Sophie's expression softened slightly, though she didn't drop her guard entirely. "Why are you really here, Ethan?"

Second Chances

He took a slow breath. "Because I don't want this to be the end of us."

Her eyes narrowed. "There was never an 'us.' You lied to me, you hid who you were, and you used me as a way to—"

"I was wrong," Ethan interrupted, his voice firm but not angry. "I've made mistakes, Sophie. More than I can count. But that doesn't change what I feel for you."

She blinked, caught off guard. "Feel for me?"

"Yes," he said simply. "You've challenged me, made me see the world differently. You've forced me to question everything I thought I knew. I know I don't deserve your forgiveness, but I want the chance to prove to you that I'm not the man I was."

Sophie's lips parted as if to respond, but she closed them again, her brows furrowing. For a moment, she seemed to weigh his words, her sharp mind analyzing, calculating. Then she looked away, her gaze sweeping across the ballroom before returning to him.

"I don't trust you," she said quietly.

"I understand," Ethan replied. "But trust can be rebuilt. If you're willing to give me that chance."

She shook her head slightly, as if trying to clear her thoughts. "You think it's that simple? That you can just show up and say the right things, and I'll forget everything that happened?"

The Secret Private Driver

"No," Ethan said. "I think it's going to take time. And I think it's going to be hard. But I'm willing to put in that work if you'll let me."

Sophie stared at him, her expression unreadable. Finally, she spoke. "I don't know, Ethan. I don't know if I can do this again."

"I'm not asking for anything right now," he said softly. "I just wanted you to know how I feel. And to tell you that I'll be here, if and when you're ready."

She didn't respond immediately. Instead, she turned her gaze back to the crowd, her posture still guarded. But Ethan thought he saw something shift in her stance, a slight relaxation of her shoulders, a softening of the tension that had been there since the moment he arrived.

When Sophie finally looked at him again, her eyes held a flicker of something he hadn't seen before. It wasn't forgiveness, not yet. But it wasn't dismissal either.

"Ethan," she said, her voice quieter now, "if I even consider giving you that chance, you're going to have to prove it to me. Over and over again."

"I understand," he said, his voice steady. "And I will."

She held his gaze for a long moment, then nodded once. "We'll see."

It wasn't a yes. It wasn't a no. But it was something. And for

Second Chances

Ethan, that was enough to hold onto.

As the evening continued, they didn't speak again, but they lingered in each other's orbit, their paths crossing subtly as the night went on. It was a start. And for the first time in a long time, Ethan felt a glimmer of hope.

Eighteen

Grand Gesture

It was nearly midnight when Ethan Steele stood alone in the dimly lit studio, the only sounds coming from the muffled rush of traffic outside and the occasional creak of the building settling in the cold night air. The room had a lived-in feel: papers scattered across desks, camera equipment haphazardly stashed in corners, and a faint smell of stale coffee lingering in the air. This was Sophie Carter's domain—the beating heart of her investigative work.

He had come here unannounced, knowing full well the risk. It wasn't a grand stage, a glittering ballroom, or a corporate boardroom. It was Sophie's world, one that didn't yield to flashy words or sweeping gestures. She had stripped him down to his core once before, demanding honesty, forcing him to face truths he'd long buried. And now, if there was any hope of bridging the growing chasm between them, it had to start here.

Grand Gesture

Ethan turned the small flash drive over in his hand. Its metallic surface reflected the dim light, the object feeling heavier than it was. This wasn't just another data dump. It wasn't an olive branch. It was everything—his empire's inner workings, the names, the documents, the proof. And most importantly, it was something she didn't yet know existed: the one piece of evidence that might change everything.

The door creaked open, and Sophie stepped in, her movements brisk. She was bundled in a long coat, her scarf loosely draped around her neck, and her expression was guarded the moment she saw him. She stopped just inside, letting the door close behind her with a soft click.

"You shouldn't be here," she said, her voice low, calm, and utterly unwelcoming.

Ethan's lips pressed into a thin line. "I know."

"So why are you?"

He held up the flash drive. "Because there's more you need to see."

Sophie let out a short laugh, devoid of humor. She shrugged off her coat, draping it over a chair, then leaned back against the desk with crossed arms. "You want to feed me another leak, Ethan? Another carefully chosen set of files to steer the narrative?"

"No." His tone was even. "This time, it's everything. No filters,

The Secret Private Driver

no omissions. The whole truth."

She narrowed her eyes. "You already said you gave me everything. Why should I believe there's more?"

"Because I was afraid," he admitted, his voice steady but carrying an edge of vulnerability. "Afraid of what would happen if you knew the full extent. Afraid of how far it went—of who would get hurt. And if I'm being honest, I was afraid of what you'd think of me."

Sophie's arms dropped to her sides. "You really expect me to believe that?"

He took a step closer, holding out the flash drive. "I don't expect you to believe anything. I'm just asking you to look at it. To decide for yourself."

Her gaze flicked between the drive and his face, skepticism written all over her features. "And what happens after I look at it? You want me to keep this quiet? To give you a pass on the damage it might cause?"

Ethan shook his head. "No. I'm not asking you to protect me. Whatever you find in there, you can do what you want with it. Publish it, destroy it, confront me—your choice."

Sophie's expression softened slightly, though her voice remained sharp. "What's the catch?"

"There isn't one," he said, his tone calm but insistent. "I need you to have the whole story, not just the pieces I was willing to give you before."

For a long moment, neither of them spoke. The air between them felt charged, the weight of their shared history hanging heavily. Sophie finally stepped forward, slowly reaching for the flash drive. Her fingers brushed his as she took it, and she quickly stepped back, holding it in her palm as though it might burn her.

"Why now?" she asked quietly.

"Because I can't move forward until you know the truth. All of it."

Sophie tilted her head slightly, studying him. "What are you really hoping for here, Ethan? Redemption? Forgiveness? You think this changes what you did?"

"No," he said, his voice low. "I don't think it changes the past. But I'm hoping it changes how you see me now."

Her breath caught for a brief moment, though she quickly masked it. She turned away, moving to her desk, where she inserted the flash drive into her laptop. Ethan stayed where he was, his hands in his pockets, watching her closely.

The room filled with the soft hum of the computer's fan, the glow from the screen casting shadows across her face. Sophie's brow furrowed as she clicked through the files, her eyes scanning the endless rows of data, the confidential memos, the transaction logs. Her face shifted—confusion, recognition, and finally something that looked like shock.

She turned back to him, her voice quieter now, but still sharp. "These accounts... they're connected to—"

"Yes," Ethan said, cutting her off before she could say the name aloud. "I found them after I stepped down. They weren't in the original audit because they were hidden behind several layers of shell corporations."

"And you're giving me this?" she asked, incredulous. "Do you have any idea what this means? Who this implicates?"

"I do," Ethan said simply.

Sophie leaned back, running a hand through her hair. "This is bigger than Steele Industries. This is—"

"It's everything," Ethan finished. "And it's why I couldn't hold it back any longer. You deserve to know. The world deserves to know."

Sophie turned back to the screen, her hands hovering over the keyboard as she stared at the information before her. Ethan could see the gears turning in her mind, the pieces coming together. This was her world—piecing together fragments of a puzzle until the bigger picture emerged. But he also knew what this meant for her, the pressure it would put on her shoulders.

Finally, she turned back to him, her voice quieter now, almost weary. "If I run this, it's going to tear apart more than just your company."

Ethan nodded. "I know."

"And you're okay with that?"

"I'm not okay with it," he admitted. "But it's necessary."

Sophie studied him for a long moment, then turned back to the laptop. "You're not the man I thought you were."

"I know that too," he said. "I just hope I'm someone you can believe in again."

Her hands stilled on the keyboard. She didn't look at him, didn't say anything more. But the fact that she didn't tell him to leave, didn't tell him to take back the flash drive, was enough for Ethan.

He stepped toward the door, his voice quiet as he said, "Whatever you decide, I'll respect it."

As he slipped out into the cold night air, leaving Sophie alone with the files that could reshape everything, he felt a flicker of hope. It wasn't much. But it was a start.

Nineteen

Price of the Truth

Sophie Carter felt the weight of the flash drive in her pocket as she walked into the newsroom the following morning. The bustling open floor plan of The Ledger was alive with the usual symphony of ringing phones, hurried footsteps, and the steady click-clack of keyboards. For years, this place had been her second home—a space where she'd broken stories that toppled mayors, exposed corporate fraud, and earned her respect as one of the fiercest investigative journalists in the city.

But today, her steps were heavier, her chest tight with the gravity of what she carried. This wasn't just another exposé. The information Ethan Steele had given her wasn't just a continuation of the story she had already told. It was a bombshell that would ripple far beyond Steele Industries, exposing a level of corruption that reached into corners of power she hadn't dared imagine.

She reached her desk and sat down, pulling out the drive and placing it on the worn wood surface. Its silver exterior caught the morning light streaming through the tall windows, making it appear almost innocent. But Sophie knew better. Inside were documents implicating not only Ethan's former board members but also high-ranking government officials, well-known philanthropists, and even certain rival CEOs who had publicly condemned Steele Industries after her initial article.

She opened her laptop, her fingers trembling as she inserted the drive. The files sprang to life on the screen, each folder a door to another scandal. Emails outlining secret meetings, memos hinting at hush money payments, contracts that contradicted public statements—every piece meticulously documented, waiting for her to piece it all together.

But it wasn't just the content that made her hesitate. It was the source. Ethan Steele, the man she had built a career on exposing, had handed her this information. He had claimed to want to come clean, to make amends. Yet Sophie couldn't shake the nagging suspicion that there was more to his motives. Was he trying to use her, once again, to take down his rivals? Or was he truly ready to let the truth come out, no matter the cost?

The questions gnawed at her as she began to comb through the files. She traced financial transactions that led to offshore accounts, linked names on corporate letterhead to shell companies, and highlighted inconsistencies in official statements

The Secret Private Driver

made by public figures. Every piece of evidence fit together too perfectly, almost as if Ethan had spent years assembling this puzzle, waiting for the right moment to hand it over.

As she worked, Sophie felt a chill run down her spine. This wasn't just a story that would make headlines—it was one that could bring down giants. It would rattle the foundations of trust in major institutions, spark investigations that could drag on for years, and almost certainly put her in the crosshairs of powerful people who had everything to lose.

Her phone buzzed, pulling her out of her thoughts. She glanced at the screen. A text from Ethan.

Ethan: Have you started looking at it?

Sophie hesitated before typing back.

Sophie: I'm reviewing it now.

His response came almost immediately.

Ethan: Be careful. Some of the people involved won't take kindly to this coming out.

She stared at the message, her heart racing. It wasn't a threat—she was certain of that. But it was a warning, one she couldn't ignore.

Her editor's voice snapped her out of her thoughts. "Carter! Got a minute?"

Price of the Truth

She closed her laptop and turned to see Jim Henderson standing by her desk, a mug of coffee in one hand and a notepad in the other. He was a gruff, no-nonsense man who'd been in the business long enough to recognize a career-defining story when he saw one. But she wasn't ready to loop him in—not yet.

"Yeah, what's up?" she said, forcing a casual tone.

"You're working on something big again, aren't you?" He squinted at her, as if he could see the secrets written across her face. "I can tell."

"Just following a lead," Sophie said noncommittally. "Nothing solid yet."

Jim raised an eyebrow but didn't push. "Well, don't take too long. We've got a lot of eyes on us after that Steele piece. If there's another bombshell, I want us to be the ones to drop it."

"I'll keep you posted," Sophie promised, though her stomach churned at the thought of how much more explosive this new story would be.

As Jim walked away, Sophie turned back to her laptop. The weight of the decision ahead felt suffocating. If she ran with this, she would be exposing not just Steele Industries but an entire network of corruption. She would be painting a target on her back. And she would be placing her trust in a man she had every reason to doubt.

Hours passed as she worked, the newsroom bustling around her.

She jotted notes, cross-referenced sources, and constructed a timeline that made her skin crawl. By the time the sun dipped below the horizon, casting long shadows across the room, Sophie had a clearer picture of what she was dealing with—and it terrified her.

She leaned back in her chair, staring at the wall of notes and printouts she had pinned up. The evidence was airtight, the narrative undeniable. But with every step forward, she felt the ground beneath her shift. The closer she got to publishing, the more she realized how far-reaching the consequences would be.

Her phone buzzed again. Another message from Ethan.

Ethan: If you need help, you know where to find me.

Sophie let the phone fall to the desk, her head in her hands. For all his faults, Ethan had shown a level of transparency she hadn't expected. He had offered her the truth on a silver platter, knowing it would likely destroy him. But trusting him completely was something she couldn't bring herself to do.

As the night wore on, Sophie's resolve hardened. The truth mattered. It had always mattered. And no matter the risks, no matter the fallout, she knew she had to tell this story. But she also knew she couldn't do it alone.

She picked up her phone and dialed Jim's number. When he answered, she took a deep breath and said, "Jim, I've got something. Something big."

The silence on the other end was brief but telling. "How big?" he asked.

"Bigger than Steele Industries. Bigger than anything we've ever run before."

"Alright," Jim said, his tone steady. "Let's talk."

As Sophie ended the call and turned back to her laptop, she knew there was no turning back. This wasn't just about exposing corruption anymore. It was about facing the fallout, risking everything, and trusting herself—and maybe, just maybe, trusting Ethan—to see it through.

Twenty

Shadows

Ethan Steele sat in the corner of a small café in Midtown, a cup of untouched coffee cooling on the table in front of him. The late afternoon sun filtered weakly through the plate glass windows, casting long, muted shadows. He glanced around the café, scanning faces, noting movements, assessing his surroundings. The patrons were ordinary—business people grabbing late lunches, students huddled over laptops, a couple quietly arguing at a table near the counter. On the surface, nothing seemed out of the ordinary.

But Ethan's instincts told him otherwise. He could feel the weight of eyes on him, subtle but present. Maybe it was paranoia; maybe it wasn't. It didn't matter. Paranoia was what had kept him alive through years of playing high-stakes games behind corporate walls.

Shadows

A faint buzz vibrated against his palm, and Ethan looked down at his phone. The message was short, simple.

Sophie: We need to talk. Tonight.

His chest tightened. He hadn't heard from her since she'd started digging into the files he'd handed over. He knew she was probably drowning in data, making connections he'd never dared to pursue. She was the one person he could trust to put it all together, to see it through. And yet, knowing what she was uncovering—what it might cost both of them—made the hours crawl by like days.

Ethan typed back, keeping his reply equally brief.

Ethan: Where?

He waited, staring at the screen until her response appeared.

Sophie: Your place. Eight o'clock.

He slid the phone into his pocket and left a twenty on the table before heading out. As he stepped onto the street, the chill of early evening air brushed his face. The city felt different tonight. More restless. People moved briskly, their faces drawn tight, their conversations muted. It could have been his imagination, but the energy in the air felt charged—like the seconds before a storm breaks.

—-

The Secret Private Driver

Ethan's penthouse felt cavernous as he stepped inside, the heavy door clicking shut behind him. The sprawling windows revealed a sweeping view of the city, its lights flickering against the encroaching darkness. He moved through the space like a ghost, his mind already racing ahead to the conversation he was about to have. Sophie was relentless—he knew that. Once she decided on a course of action, nothing would stop her.

It was one of the reasons he respected her. And one of the reasons she terrified him.

At exactly eight o'clock, the intercom buzzed. Ethan crossed to the panel, pressing the button.

"Come up."

A few moments later, Sophie stepped off the elevator and into his penthouse. She looked both calm and restless, her coat slung over one arm, her bag weighing heavily on her shoulder. She didn't waste time on pleasantries.

"You said this was everything," she said, her tone sharp.

"It was," Ethan replied evenly. "It is."

Sophie dropped her bag onto the nearest chair and pulled out a thick stack of printouts. She slammed them down on the marble countertop. "Then why do I keep finding threads that lead to even deeper holes?"

Ethan frowned. "What are you talking about?"

"These accounts," she said, flipping through the pages. "The ones you flagged in the offshore files. They're tied to a company that doesn't officially exist. No records, no incorporation documents—just a name. And that name keeps showing up on contracts with Steele Industries and half a dozen other firms."

Ethan felt a knot form in his stomach. "That shouldn't be possible. I traced everything—"

"Not far enough," Sophie cut in. "Whoever set this up was good. Layers of shell companies, fake directors, dummy accounts. But I've seen patterns like this before. Someone's covering their tracks, and they're doing it so well that even you missed it."

He stepped closer, scanning the documents she laid out. The names, the transactions, the timeline—it was all there. And she was right. He hadn't seen it before, but now it was glaringly obvious. This wasn't just his company's corruption. It went deeper, reaching into entities he hadn't even known existed.

"This isn't just Steele Industries," Sophie said, her voice low. "This is something much bigger. And if I'm right, the people behind it won't just try to bury it. They'll bury anyone who gets too close."

Ethan looked up at her, his eyes narrowing. "You think you're in danger?"

"I think we're both in danger," she said. "And I think the people pulling the strings aren't going to let this come out without a fight."

A heavy silence fell between them. The gravity of the situation was clear. They weren't just dealing with corporate greed or regulatory violations. This was organized, deliberate, and calculated. The kind of operation that didn't just rely on NDAs and lawsuits to keep people quiet.

Ethan took a step back, running a hand through his hair. "Why did you come here?"

"Because I need to know if you're in this all the way," Sophie said, her voice steady but tinged with urgency. "If I keep digging, if I keep connecting these dots, it's not just my reputation on the line. I need to know if you're going to back me when things get dangerous."

He met her gaze, and for the first time, he saw something in her eyes that wasn't just determination. It was fear. Not for herself, but for what this story might unleash.

"I'm with you," he said quietly. "All the way."

She nodded, her shoulders relaxing ever so slightly. "Good. Because we're going to need every bit of leverage we can get."

They spent the next few hours going through the files together, identifying patterns, marking connections, building a roadmap of the sprawling network they were uncovering. The deeper they went, the clearer it became that this was no ordinary scandal. This was systemic. Pervasive. And incredibly dangerous.

Shadows

As the clock struck midnight, Sophie leaned back in her chair, rubbing her temples. "This is going to be a war."

Ethan stood, looking out over the city, his reflection faint in the glass. "Then we'll fight it."

She watched him for a moment, her expression unreadable. "You sure you're ready for that?"

He turned to face her, his eyes steady. "I have to be. Because if we don't see this through, no one else will."

Sophie nodded, her resolve hardening. "Then let's get to work."

And so they did. In the quiet hours of the night, with the city stretching out before them, they pieced together the story that would change everything. But even as they worked, Ethan couldn't shake the feeling that the shadows were closing in. That the forces they were about to expose were already watching, waiting for the moment to strike.

When Sophie finally packed her bag and headed toward the elevator, Ethan walked her to the door. As the elevator doors closed, he stood there in the dim light of his penthouse, the faint hum of the city below like a warning in the distance.

He didn't know what would happen next. But he knew one thing for certain.

They were in this together now. And there was no turning back.

www.ingramcontent.com/pod-product-compliance
Lightning Source LLC
LaVergne TN
LVHW020441070526
838199LV00063B/4806